Women *of* Courage

by Donna Kafer

Bridge-Logos
Orlando, FL 32822 USA

Bridge-Logos

Orlando, FL 32822 USA

Women of Courage
by Donna Kafer

Copyright ©2007 by Bridge-Logos

Printed in Canada.

Library of Congress Catalog Card Number: 2007931032
ISBN: 978-0-88270-345-9

Unless otherwise noted, all Scripture notations are taken from the *King James Version* (KJV) of the Bible.

G532.316.N.m706.35250

Dedication

To the women who have left an indelible impression on my life:

My Mother: Doris Elizabeth Hamilton: Because of your love for learning and reading I was influenced at a very young age to read and develop an interest in people and history. Thank you for inspiring me to appreciate the written word that opened the world to my curiosity.

My Mother-in-Law: Ruth Schuster Kafer: Your love of family, friends and fun have always been an inspiration to me, but it is your good fight against illness that offers me the opportunity to see grace in action.

My Daughter: Andrea Elizabeth Kafer: A true gift from God—fun, bright and loving. Thank you for who you are and who you are becoming. May God bless you at every turn of your life and inspire you to be a woman who has the "impression" of the living God on your life.

To my Hero: Ross Stephen Kafer, my husband, my friend, my encourager for this life's journey. Thank you for your patience and perseverance with me during this writing process. You have always believed in me, and I love and cherish you very much.

God bless!

Chaplain
Donna
Kafer

Romans
12:12

Contents

Courage through Loss

Introduction

Throughout the history of the world there has been much recorded concerning the great achievements of notable women—women who have accomplished many critical and thought-provoking wonders for mankind. However, most history books do not share the faith of the amazing women who have shaped families, nations and governments through the power and love of Jesus Christ.

God never intended for woman to stay behind veiled curtains, locked away from the world. Instead woman was placed on earth when Adam soon realized that his life was incomplete, and that he needed a helpmeet for the journey.

God intended that man would recognize this void, and when woman graced our small planet, man was blessed indeed. Eve came to show the world that without her, life would be nonexistent and far less beautiful.

Granted Eve sinned and mankind fell into destruction, but because man was culpable as well, the stage was thus set to bring deliverance to the world through the seed of a woman. (Genesis 3:15)

In many societies and cultures around the world, women have been and still are little more than possessions to be bought and traded, a far cry from what our heavenly Father intended for the life of women. Instead He designed them to be compassionate nurturers and teachers that would leave a significant, lasting impression on their husbands, children and world.

Women of Courage explores the lives of ordinary women who defied the odds, counted the cost, and took up their cross to overcome difficult and trying times that could have crushed them. Through their faith in Christ they persevered against all odds, gaining:

- Courage for Suffering & Injustice
- Courage for the Great Commission
- Courage Through Loss

Each woman grew into a "display of His splendor" in what we call "Gardens of Grace." May their stories nourish your faith for the journey that lies ahead to "grow in grace and in the knowledge of our Lord and Savior Jesus Christ" (2 Peter 3:18).

PART ONE

Courage

through

Suffering

and

Injustice

THEREFORE, THERE IS NOW
NO CONDEMNATION FOR THOSE
WHO ARE IN CHRIST JESUS.

ROMANS 8:1

BE STRONG AND COURAGEOUS.
DO NOT BE AFRAID OR
TERRIFIED BECAUSE OF THEM,
FOR THE LORD YOUR GOD
GOES WITH YOU;
HE WILL NEVER LEAVE YOU
NOR FORSAKE YOU.

DEUTERONOMY 31:6

Introduction to
Part One

Courage Through
Suffering and Injustice

As women we know all too well the severe injustices that have and are being committed against women, children and the poor in the world. We shudder and cringe at the news reports concerning child abductions, child abuse, sexual assaults and scenes of starving children flashing across our screens. From the severe punishments and maddening social injustices in the Far and Middle East to the limitations of equal pay for equal work in the West, we understand that as women we will always endure hardships. Of course comparing the dilemma of a child widow in India forced to live the rest of her life in an Ashram to the wrangling for an increase in salary for a corporate single mom is not exactly equal, but we still share in the universal struggle that only women understand.

Because we are created to be nurturers and compassionate caretakers, we are naturally drawn to champion the causes of those facing social injustice, as well as helping those who are suffering from all manner of ills. Our call to combat injustice and overcome suffering may come from many different and diverse areas of the world. Some may feel called to the nations that are faced with starvation or those trying to recover from devastating illnesses such as AIDS. You may be called to protect children, ease the despair of those women languishing in prison or even provide shelter for the homeless and mentally ill that roam our streets—but we are all called to ease the pain and suffering of the world.

What does the Bible have to say about the injustice and suffering of the world? Not just injustice against women or the suffering of children, but injustice against all mankind? We know that Jesus understood the suffering of the multitudes, of those who were afflicted or in distress, whether it was from physical ailments or other types of suffering. He had a heart for the displaced unloved people of his day and He sought to alleviate their pain, to help them in their daily struggles. In James 1:27 we read, "Religion that God our Father accepts as pure and faultless is this: to look after orphans and widows in their distress and to keep oneself from being polluted by the world." Our reaction to injustice should be immediate and our hearts should be filled with mercy for those who suffer from poverty, hunger and imprisonment.

In Isaiah 58 we hear God speaking through His prophet Isaiah concerning the people's so called desire to draw closer to God and His apparent silence as a response to their efforts. God knew that they were not really sincere in their fasts because of their behavior towards Him during their days of fasting. God makes it clear in Isaiah 58:6-7 which type of fast he loves, a fast motivated by sincere faith and obedience to His moral law: "Is not this the kind of fasting I have chosen: to loose the chains of injustice and untie the cords of the yoke, to set the oppressed free and break every yoke? Is it not to share your food with the hungry and to provide the poor wanderer with shelter—when you see the naked, to clothe him, and not to turn away from your own flesh and blood?"

Did Jesus not say it best this way?: *"For I was hungry and you gave me something to eat, I was thirsty and you gave me something to drink, I was a stranger and you invited me in, I needed clothes and you clothed me, I was sick and you looked after me, I was in prison and you came to visit me"* (Matthew 25:35-36). How precious is our Savior! He looks after all of us and then we look after the world and he tells us that as we are to *bless Him* by caring for others. What a joy to be able to minister to our beautiful Savior!

Through these true life stories of women who answered the call and made a difference in the world, we too can see the call of Christ on our lives to aid those who need an advocate for social injustice or suffering. May you see the need of others and answer the call to *minister personally to Jesus as He is personally ministering to you.*

THE TULIP PROVIDES SUCH STUNNING BEAUTY IT IS DIFFICULT TO
BELIEVE IT COMES FROM A HARD BULB PLANTED IN THE COLD FALL SOIL.
BUT IN THE NEWNESS OF SPRING, IT BURSTS FORTH IN GLORIOUS COLOR.
CORRIE TEN BOOM'S FAITHFULNESS AND COURAGE DISPLAYS THE
ESSENCE OF THE LOVELY TULIP.

Corrie Ten Boom

1892–1983

Hid Jews from the Nazis

Cornelia Johanna Arnalda Ten Boom was born in 1892 to a loving, Christian family in Amsterdam, the Netherlands. Shortly after Corrie's birth, her parents decided to move into the center of Amsterdam and open a small jewelry store. This little jewelry store was in a narrow house right in the heart of the Jewish section known as Haarlam.

Living in the midst of the Jewish community gave Corrie and her family many opportunities to interact with the people who frequented their jewelry store. The Ten Booms were invited to participate in their Sabbath and join with them in their feasts and celebrations. They enjoyed studying the Old Testament together and were very happy to share their lives with their wonderful Jewish friends.

Corrie's family were members of the Dutch Reformed Church. Her father was a kind man who was friends with half of the city of Haarlam; and her mother was known for her kindness and compassion towards others before her death from a stroke. With their strong faith lived out in their daily lives, it was only natural that the Ten Booms began taking in children beginning in 1918. Though their house was very small, their hearts were much bigger and brimming with love.

In 1920, Corrie began training as a watchmaker and became the first female watchmaker licensed in the Netherlands in 1922. She was a very active and social young woman and in 1923 she helped organize the first girls' club. Subsequently these clubs grew in the 1930s to become the very large Triangle Club.

Growing up in a family of strong, compassionate Christians provided Corrie with many examples of service and mercy towards others. In a story she recounts crediting her father's inspiring example in helping the Jews of Holland, she recalled an incident in which she asked a pastor who was visiting their home to help shield a woman and a new born infant. He replied, "No definitely not. We could lose our lives for that." She went on to say, "Unseen by either of us, father had appeared in the door, 'Give the child to me, Corrie,' he said. Father held the baby close, his white beard brushing its cheek, looking into the little face with eyes as blue and innocent as the baby's. 'If we could lose our lives for this child, I would consider that the greatest honor that could come to my family.'" (*The Hiding Place*, p.99)

Corrie never married. She lived with her father and older sister Betsy, working in the jewelry store, enjoying her family and friendships with her Jewish neighbors. When the Nazis invaded Holland in 1940 Corrie was 48 years old, and when the Nazis began forcing the Jews from their homes she began to take them in temporarily until she could find them places to stay in the countryside. Soon the word spread that the Ten Boom house was a safe refuge and many more began showing up seeking shelter. No matter how quickly she found homes for the families, more followed.

As the situation grew even more critical, Corrie had a false wall constructed in her bedroom where people could hide. These events continued for a year and a half, her home becoming the central headquarters for an underground ring that reached throughout the Netherlands. The Ten Boom family only wanted to help the Jewish people—they were not trying to convert them. They allowed them to honor the Sabbath and even provided Kosher food. Times were desperate as dozens of displaced Jews came in and out of the small watch shop looking for places to stay. Corrie found herself handling reports, appeals, and hundreds of ration cards a month that went to help feed the Jews that were hiding in all the underground homes across Holland. Corrie began to wonder just how long this much activity could go unnoticed by the Germans, and how long they could continue to hide seven Jews in their own home and keep it a secret.

That time finally came on February 28, 1944, when a man came into their shop and asked Corrie to help him free his wife, who had been arrested for hiding Jews. He desperately needed a hundred gilders to bribe a policeman for her freedom. Ten Boom promised to help, finding out later that he was what the Nazis called a *quisling*, an informant that had worked with them from the first day of the occupation. This man, Jan Vogel (Corrie later learned), turned their family in to the Gestapo, who then raided their home later in the day, arresting Corrie and her family. Thankfully, the Jews that were in their home were able to make it to the hiding place undiscovered and eventually were able to escape to a new location.

Corrie's father died from an illness within ten days of his arrest, never to see his daughters again. The two sisters were first sent to Scheveningen concentration camp, then to the Vught political concentration camp (both in the Netherlands) and finally to the notorious Ravensbruck concentration camp in Germany.

Corrie relates in her book, *The Hiding Place*, how she struggled with the hate she felt for the man who had turned her family in and how much she hated the Nazis for their evil. But her dear sister Betsie always reminded her of how much Jesus loved the Germans and would want them to pray for them and ask God to forgive them. For Corrie this was too much to ask. Their father had died, and now even her sister had become very ill. She watched as Betsie lost weight, and in spite of her sister's attempt to encourage her to forgive, she felt only ill will for her captors.

The times that Corrie was able to rally her faith were when she and Betsie gave comfort to the other prisoners. She relates a typical evening in which they would use their prized, secreted Bible to hold worship services:

"At first Betsie and I called these meetings with great timidity, but as night after night went by and no guard ever came near us, we grew bolder. There were so many that longed to join us, we decided to hold a second service after the evening roll call. These services were like no others, these times in Barracks 28. There were so many from different faiths in attendance, we might have a recitation Magnificent in Latin by a group of Roman Catholics, a whispered hymn by some Lutherans and a *sotto-voce* chant by Eastern Orthodox women. With each moment the crowd would swell, packing the nearby platforms, hanging over the edges, until the high steps groaned and swayed. Barracks 28 became known throughout the camp as 'the crazy place where they hope.'"

When the women complained about the lice and fleas that crawled all over them, Betsie reminded them that they should be thankful for everything, even the vermin. "How can we?" they grumbled. "They make us itch all over."

Betsie smiled and nodded knowingly, "They are the reason that the guards stay away from our worship time. They don't want to be bitten by the fleas and lice."

With that thought, all the women gave thanks for the fleas and lice that kept the guards away as they came together to worship God.

Betsie's health continued to worsen, and Corrie became deeply grieved for all her sister was enduring. But Betsie continued to encourage her sister, lovingly reminding her that Jesus would want them to pray. It was difficult to find forgiveness in her heart for their captors when they abused them and humiliated them by making them stand naked for role call in the early morning cold.

As Betsie grew steadily weaker her last words to Corrie were, "[We] must tell them what we have learned here. We must tell them that there is no pit so deep that He is not deeper still. They will listen, Corrie, because we have been here."

Betsie died on December 16, 1944. Corrie, who had prayed with Betsie the day before for her to be healed, could not understand how God could have let this happen. Hadn't Betsie even said with confidence, "Yes, the Lord will heal me"?

"They laid her thin body on the concrete floor along with all the other corpses of the women who died that day, and it was hard for me to understand, to believe that God had a purpose for all that. Yet because of Betsie's death, today I am traveling all over the world telling people about Jesus."

Corrie was released from Ravensbruck on December 31, 1944, due to a clerical error—one week before she and all the other women her age were to be killed. Corrie remembered the day she was released as if it were yesterday:

"'Follow me,' a young girl in an officer's uniform said to me. I walked slowly through the gate, never looking back. Behind me I heard the hinges squeak as the gate swung shut. I was free and flooding through my mind were the words of Jesus to the church at Philadelphia: 'Behold, I have set before thee an open door, and no man can shut it...' (Revelation 3:8).

"Only to those who have been in prison does freedom have such great meaning. When you are dying—when you stand at the gate of eternity—you will see things from a different perspective than when you think you may live for a long time. I [stood] at the gate for many months, living in Barracks 28, in the shadow of the crematorium. Every time I saw smoke pouring from the hideous smokestacks I knew it was the last remains of some poor woman who had been in Ravensbruck. Often I asked myself, 'When will it be my time to be killed or die?'"

After traveling back to Haarlam on a three-day journey, filthy, gaunt and weak, Corrie tried for a while to return to her profession as a watchmaker. But she found that she was no longer content doing that type of work. Instead she began traveling and telling the story of her family and what she and Betsie had learned in the concentration camp. Eventually, after the war was over, she was able to obtain permission to allow former inmates to come and hear her and find healing from their experiences.

Corrie also had a healing in her life through an incident that happened after she had been preaching in Germany in 1947. It was then that she was approached by one of the cruelest former Ravensbruck camp guards.

"And I stood there—I who had every day sins to be forgiven—and could not. Betsie had died in that place—could he erase her slow terrible death simply for the asking? It could not have been many seconds that he stood there, hand held out, but to me it seemed hours as I wrestled with the most difficult thing I had ever had to do. For I had to do it—I knew that. The message that God forgives has a prior condition: that we forgive those who have injured us. 'If you do not forgive men their trespasses,' Jesus says, 'neither will your Father in heaven forgive your trespass.' And still I stood there with the coldness clutching my heart. But forgiveness is not an emotion—I knew that too. Forgiveness is an act of the will, and the will can function regardless of the temperature of the heart. 'Jesus, help me!' I prayed silently, 'I can lift my hand, I can do that much. You supply the feeling.'

"And so woodenly, mechanically, I thrust my hand into the one stretched out to me, and as I did, an incredible thing took place. The current started in my shoulder, raced down my arm, sprang into our joined hands. And then this healing warmth seemed to flood my whole being, bringing tears to my eyes.

"'I forgive you brother!' I cried. 'With all my heart!'

"For a long moment we grasped each other's hands, the former guard and the former prisoner. I had never known God as intensely as I did then."

Corrie Ten Boom was honored by the State of Israel for her work in aid of the Jewish people by being invited to plant a tree in the Avenue of the Righteous Gentiles, at the Yad Vashem, near Jerusalem.

Ten Boom was knighted by the Queen of Holland in recognition of her work during the war. A museum in Haarlam, the city in the Netherlands in which she grew up and spent much of her life, is dedicated to her and her family.

Corrie Ten Boom passed away in Orange, California, due to a series of successive strokes that left her an invalid. She died on April 15, 1983, on her 91st birthday. It has been reported that just before dying she said she was happy to die on her birthday to be able to "celebrate it with the Lord."

Scripture Application

> IF YOU ARE INSULTED
> BECAUSE OF THE
> NAME OF CHRIST,
> YOU ARE BLESSED,
> FOR THE SPIRIT
> OF GLORY
> AND OF GOD
> RESTS ON YOU.
>
> 1 PETER 4:14

IRON CROSS FLOWER
IN THE CENTER OF THIS HUMBLE FLOWER YOU WILL SEE BEAUTY THAT
ISN'T NOTICED AT FIRST GLANCE. A CROSS REVEALS ITSELF, CREATING
AN IMMEDIATE RECOGNITION OF THE DIVINE HAND OF GOD. MOTHER
TERESA'S LIFE WAS A PERFECT EXAMPLE OF THE MASTER'S TOUCH, HUMBLY
CARING FOR THE POOR WITH UNDYING LOVE.

Mother Teresa

1910–1997

Founder of
Missionaries of Charities Order

Agnes Gonxha Bojaxhiu was born in Skopje Macedonia (formerly Yugoslavia) the youngest of three children to a family of Albanian descent. Agnes knew by the age of twelve that God had called her to become a missionary and share the love of Christ with the world. As a teen she became involved in a youth group in her local parish, called Sodality. The group was led by a Jesuit Priest who guided all their activities and from that involvement Agnes became interested in missionary work. Young Agnes enjoyed all forms of participation at her church, from lively discussions with her youth group to singing in the choir. Music was so much a part of her life that she joined the Albanian Catholic Choir and even learned to play the mandolin.

Nikola and Drana Bojaxhiu, Agnes' parents, had settled in Skopje just after the turn of the century where her father co-owned a construction firm that provided his family with all the necessary comforts of life. Agnes' father had been involved in politics and his premature death in either 1918 or 1919 provoked some speculation that he might have been poisoned by political rivals. Her brother Lazar is quoted as saying, "When Yugoslavia took over the territories the family was persecuted and my father poisoned." Whether there was any truth in that statement has been widely disputed, but interesting to note. Her mother, Dranafile (meaning Rose) may have been of Italian descent although some reports indicate her family may have owned land in Serbia. Her mother was not interested in politics and after her husband's early death she spoke about religion more often and their ties to the local church was strengthened.

When Agnes decided to give her life to the service of God she told her brother Lazar, a lieutenant in the Albanian army, but his reaction was not that enthusiastic. Later in a letter to him she simply stated, "You will serve a king of two million people, I shall serve the King of the whole world." But by this time she had applied and been accepted to join the Sisters of Loreto, an Irish order of nuns that had been established in the seventeenth century. After a few moths of training in Dublin, the order sent her to the city of Darjeeling in northeast India. It was there on May 24, 1931 that Agnes took her initial vows as a nun and thoughtfully chose the name of Teresa in honor of St. Teresa of Lisieux.

Having been assigned to teach geography and catechism at St. Mary's High School for Girls in Calcutta, south of Darjeeling, Sister Teresa soon proved her worth as an instructor. In 1944, she became principle of the school and not too long after became infected with tuberculosis and was sent to Darjeeling for rest and recuperation. It was on the train ride back to Darjeeling that

Sister Teresa took note of the beggars, lepers and the homeless that crowded the streets of Calcutta. Children and infants were often abandoned and relegated to die on the streets or in garbage bins. It was 1946 and Mother Teresa felt the second call on God's life, a calling that would change her life's work forever. She knew in her heart of hearts that God was calling her to sacrifice her life in service to the poor and needy in the slums of Calcutta. For her there was no other recourse than to resign her position in the Order of the Sisters of Loreto.

From 1931 until 1946 she had taught at St. Mary's behind convent walls, not really seeing the Calcutta she had experienced on that train ride that had impressed her so deeply. So in 1946, Mother Teresa received permission from her archbishop to begin her work helping the poor, sick and dying in the sad streets of Calcutta. Then in 1948, she received approval from Pope Piius XII to live as an independent nun. It was during this same year in December that she decided to make another big decision, becoming a citizen of India.

Even though she had no funds, she ventured out of the convent to devote her life to serving the poorest of the poor, depending on divine providence for all her needs. Opening a school for slum children in the open air, she was soon joined by others who wanted to help and the financial aid that was so needed soon became a reality. This monetary blessing enabled Mother Teresa to broaden her sphere of influence in helping those that especially needed her caring abilities. After studying nursing with Mother Dengel of the American Medical Missionaries in the Indian city of Patna, she felt better equipped to deal with those who were in all manner of poverty and illness. God was blessing her ministry indeed, and she was ready for the next step of her calling.

On October 7, 1950, Mother Teresa received permission from the Vatican to establish a Diocesan Congregation of the Calcutta Diocese, better known as the Missionary Sisters of Charity. For her habit she chose a plain white sari with a blue border and a simple cross pinned to her left shoulder. This practical "uniform" was much more suited to caring for the poor in the dusty, hot streets of Calcutta.

Of the twelve sisters that joined the order, most were former students from St. Mary's, and each one was required to devote her life to serving the poor without accepting any material reward in return. This was an additional fourth vow to the customary vows of poverty, chastity, and obedience. In addition they were not to be cloistered in a convent as tradition normally mandated, but rather allowed to live among the poor they had vowed to help and serve. Sister Teresa had now become "Mother" Teresa to those who had chosen to serve within the newly founded "Missionaries of Charity" order.

At the beginning of their work in Calcutta, Mother Teresa, Sister Agnes (the first nun to join her order) and Sister Gertrude lived at 14 Creek Lane on the upper floor of the house of Michael Gomes. Clearly they would have to pray for larger housing to be able to have the freedom they required in ministering to the poor. In 1952, Mother Teresa discovered such a place, albeit a rather unlikely prospect for furthering the Gospel of Jesus Christ. It was once used as a temple for worship of the goddess Kali, the Hindu goddess of death and destruction, but now stood abandoned and in disrepair. It was large enough to accommodate Mother Teresa's plans—she determined to convert this once pagan building into a safe haven for those who were destitute and dying in the streets of the massively overpopulated city of tears. Their prayers were answered when the Calcutta officials agreed to allow them to use a portion of the temple to care for the needs of the dying. In February 1953, twenty-seven sisters of the Missionaries of Charity moved into the three-storied building at 54A-Lower Circular Road (now Acharya Jagdish Chandra Bose Road), which was christened the Nirmal Hriday Home (which means "Pure Heart"). It eventually became known simply as the Mother House.

The Sisters of Charity immediately began to gather the dying men and women off the streets of Calcutta and into the sanctuary they had created to tend their final days on earth. Shortly after this undertaking the order set about to establish Sishu Bhavan ("Children's House") to meet the desperate needs of the unwanted, deserted babies and children. Mother Teresa was not through yet, and in 1957 the order established a center for victims of leprosy, Shanti Nagar ("The Place of Peace"), a 34-acre plot of land near the city of Asanol that was donated by the Indian government. "The Place of Peace" was a leprosarium village that consisted of a hospital, a convent, a chapel, thirty family homes and a school for their children.

The Indian government acknowledged Mother Teresa's tireless, devoted work among the people by bestowing upon her the Padmashree ("Magnificent Lotus") award in September of 1962.

Mother Teresa's boundless energy and negligible need for sleep is well reported, noting that she only needed from 3 to 4 hours a night to wake up refreshed, ready to care for others, unconcerned about her own needs. The call she felt on her life was very clear: her Jesus had asked her to serve the poor and to tend to the dying. So there was no question in her mind about what she must do in her life. She committed to being obedient to her Lord.

Pope Paul VI placed the Missionaries of Charity directly under the control of the Papacy in 1965 and authorized Mother

Teresa to expand the order outside of India. It was then that she established centers worldwide to treat lepers, the blind, the disabled, the aged, and the dying—even a center in Rome in 1968. In the mid-60s she created the companion to her organization, "The Brothers of Charity," to help run homes for the dying.

Her ultimate goal in life was to create centers wherever there was a need to care for the orphans, the poor and those in need of basic education. Mother Teresa was called to love those whom the world deemed unlovable and who the world saw as a burden to society. In her heart she knew that Jesus loved them and wanted them, so of course she must as well. For her, nothing was greater than serving Him with her entire being. She said that when she looked into the face of the one she was ministering to, she "saw the face of Jesus," and that alone motivated her to love.

Mother Teresa's goal was to serve her Jesus by tending to the needs of those who were most exposed to the neglect of the world. For her years of tireless service she received the first Pope John XXIII Peace Prize from Pope Paul VI in 1971. In the following year officials of the Indian government honored her with the Jawaharial Nehru award for International Understanding. But it was in 1979 that she received her greatest reward, the Nobel Peace Prize. Mother Teresa did not hesitate in accepting all of these awards on behalf of the poor of the world, using any money designated for the recipient to help aid her centers.

Astoundingly, by 1990 there were over 3,000 nuns who belonged to the Missionaries of Charity running centers in 25 countries, even opening a home in Russia in 1988. Not only that, but in the same year the Russian center opened, Mother Teresa visited the United States and opened a center in San Francisco

California for AIDS patients. One of her greatest joys was to be able to open a home in her native Albania in Tirana, the Capital, in 1991. By this time there were 168 homes being run by her Sisters of Charity, and later in 1995 plans were coming to fruition for several homes to be opened in China.

Mother Teresa's health was beginning to decline by the 1980s and into the 1990s, and there was much concern about her at the Vatican. While visiting Pope John Paul II in 1983 she had her first heart attack, and when in 1989 she had her second heart attack, it was nearly fatal. Fortunately she received a pacemaker and was able to continue with her ministry, not allowing her near death to slow her down at all. When at the age of 86 she became hospitalized from malaria and heart failure, the world prayed and held their breath. Her heart had stopped beating for two minutes before she was resuscitated. The physicians treating her were not so sure she would be able to recover this time. So when she awoke and asked for communion they were truly amazed. She was finally sent home just a few weeks later, in September, and a doctor stated that she firmly believed, "God will take care of me." God was truly watching over his servant, but by November she was back in the hospital where she underwent angioplasty to correct two blocked arteries. This time she was hospitalized for an entire month. It was about this same time that Mother Teresa became an honorary American citizen.

And after an eight week selection process in March of 1997, 63-year old Sister Nirmala was named as the new leader of the Missionaries of Charity. Mother Teresa had been trying to cut back on her duties for quite some time, but asked to stay on as an advisor to Sister Nirmala.

Mother Teresa had met many notables in her life, including Princess Diana whom she met on June 18, 1997, while visiting the Missionaries of Charity residence in New York. The home was in the poverty stricken area of the Bronx known as Mott Haven. The picture taken that day shows the two women holding hands, obviously enjoying their time together.

Mother Teresa celebrated her 87th birthday on August 27, and the world celebrated with her, truly loving and admiring her for all she had accomplished in her long life of devotion and service. On September 5, just 5 days after Princess Diana's tragic death from a car accident in France, Mother Teresa died of heart failure at the mission's Mother House in Calcutta.

Agnes Bonxa Bojaxhiu was a diminutive figure of a woman who was born into humble surroundings, into a family of unassuming position in life. That she rose to worldwide acclaim and adoration because of her single-minded determination to save the suffering, unloved people of the world is a testament to the resolve of one tiny woman.

As she lay dying it has been reported that her final words were "Jesus, Jesus, I love you."

Scripture Application

THEREFORE,
I URGE YOU BROTHERS,
IN VIEW OF
GOD'S MERCY,
TO OFFER YOUR BODIES
AS LIVING SACRIFICES,
HOLY AND PLEASING
TO GOD. THIS IS
YOUR SPIRITUAL
ACT OF WORSHIP.

ROMANS 12:1

THE AMERICAN BEAUTY ROSE IN ITS SPLENDOR IS UNLIKE ANY OTHER
ROSE AND WILL NEVER BE FORGOTTEN—ITS FRAGRANCE LINGERS
EVEN WHEN THE BLOOM IS GONE. ROSA PARKS IS INDELIBLY ETCHED
ON OUR HEARTS, HER LEGACY LIVES ON THROUGH TIME,
IGNITING THE SPARK OF TRUTH IN OUR OWN LIVES.

Rosa Parks

1913–2005

Mother of the
Civil Rights Movement

Rosa Louise McCauley was born on February 4, 1913 in Tuskegee, Alabama, to James and Leona McCauley. James was a carpenter by trade and Leona, a school teacher. On August 20, 1915 they welcomed Rosa's little brother Sylvester into their small family.

Sadly, James decided to strike out on his own, leaving Leona with mounting bills and no other recourse than to move with her children to her parents' small farm house in Pine Level, Alabama. It was under the care and watchful eyes of her grandfather Edwards that little Rosa learned of the terrors of the night. Each night that her grandfather slept in his rocking chair by the fireplace with a loaded rifle across his lap, Rosa would lie on the floor beside him to wait as well. Grandfather Edwards was determined that no evil would befall his family from the hands of hooded Klansman riding under the darkness of night.

Lynchings of blacks had become commonplace at the time, due to a resurgence of the Ku Klux Klan, a morbid, southern terrorist movement that was first spawned after the Civil War. This new interest was revived by filmmaker D. W. Griffith's new movie, *Birth of a Nation*. It inspired a new breed of white supremacists to twist and misinterpret his movie as a rally cry to rid American society of blacks, Jews, Catholics, and other "undesirables." They became "official" on Thanksgiving Day 1915 at Georgia's Stone Mountain, nearly a half century after the close of the Civil War. There at Stone Mountain, they raised an American flag and under the glow of a burning cross they raised their torches in a re-dedication to eradicate the "undesirables" from American soil.

Rosa would stretch out beside her grandfather's rocking chair and watch as the furtive flames from the fireplace cast dancing shadows about the darkened room. Listening to her Grandfather Edwards even breathing amidst the snap of the wood from the fire, she fought to keep her eyes open to the possibility of danger at any moment. The sound of the pounding horse's hoofs from the Klansmen riding by their small farmhouse struck terror in her heart, but she stayed because she wanted to be able to spring into action and protect her home from the white predators. Decades later Rosa explained her feelings from those nights long ago, "I remember thinking that whatever happened I wanted to see it. I wanted to see him shoot that gun."

A deep faith in God and Jesus Christ was at the heart of Rosa's upbringing and even though she faced cruelty at the hands of some whites, she was taught that you can't write off an entire race of people because of the behavior of some of its members. Rightly so she was taught that you simply cannot just turn the other cheek when people were seeking to harm or terrorize you.

It was as a little girl that Rosa experienced kindness from a myriad of whites, especially an old white woman who would take her bass fishing with craw fish tails as bait, a dear woman who treated her grandparents as equals and friends. Then there was the World War I Yankee doughboy traveling through town who patted her kindly on the head in passing, an unheard of gesture in the South. Something much more than those acts of kindness was also to affect her as she grew older. It was the immense kindness of Northern industrialists like Huntington, Rockefeller, and Carnegie who undertook the financing of many of the Tuskegee Institute's beautiful, redbrick buildings. It was from this viewpoint, seeing and appreciating the kindness that white people showed in various ways, that Rosa resolved to pray for her tormentors as they threw rocks at her and called her the ugly "N" word on her way to school.

It was her Christian faith that made her feel sorry for those who were persecuting her in their hateful ignorance. It was Psalm 23 and 27 that she had read early on that helped her find the strength to love her enemies. She had her family and the African Methodist Church to thank for her Christian foundation, learning early on that Jesus Christ is the Savior of all humankind. Her life was rooted in her Christian faith and her words speak volumes about her relationship with Christ in this quote: "I remember finding such comfort and peace while reading the Bible. Its teaching became a way of life and helped me in dealing with my day-to-day problems."

Rosa received her elementary education in an old, one room rural schoolhouse for black children that only kept its doors open five months of the year and then only going up to the sixth grade. She completed her education at the Pine Level School at the age of eleven, and then her mother Leona enrolled her in the Montgomery Industrial School for Girls, run by a Northern woman, Mrs. White. The school focused on philosophy and taught general education along with self-worth. Five years later Rosa had to leave her studies behind to return home to care for her sick grandparents. All the household duties—shopping, cooking, cleaning and caretaking—fell to young Rosa, and she did them all without complaint.

Eventually Rosa planned to continue her formal education at the Alabama State Teacher's College High School, and even though her brother Sylvester was helping by working outside the home to help pay bills, she remained in her grandparents' home to continue to care for her mother who had now become ill as well.

It wasn't until after her marriage to Raymond Parks, a barber, on December 18, 1932, that she was able to receive her high school diploma in 1934. Raymond Parks was born in Wedowee, Alabama, on February 12, 1903, and received little formal education due to the segregation laws of the time. Mr. Parks was self-educated with the help of his mother, Geri Parks. He was a smart dresser, and his thorough knowledge of domestic affairs and current events made people think he was college educated. With loving support Raymond encouraged Rosa to complete her formal education, even attending Alabama State College in Montgomery for a short time. Mrs. Parks was imbued with a strong work ethic and applied herself to a variety of different jobs over the course of her lifetime. Working as a housekeeper, seamstress and an insurance salesman, Rosa knew these were jobs that would provide the means to pursue a higher calling—the calling to end racial segregation in the United State of America.

Both Rosa and Raymond Parks became active in a variety of civil rights causes, such as voter registration. And Raymond even championed the cause to help free the "Scottsborro Boys," a well-publicized case in the 1930s. Their greatest act of service was through their work with the National Association for the Advancement of Colored People (NAACP). Because of her hard work and commitment to the NAACP, Rosa was elected to serve as secretary of the Montgomery branch and filled the role of a youth leader in later years. This group worked to dismantle the barriers of racial segregation in education and public accommodations but found little success during the 1940s and early 1950s.

In the summer of 1955, several white friends of the Parks paid expenses for Rosa to attend a two-week interracial seminar designed to help people to train for civil rights activism. This workshop was held at the Highlander Folk School in Monteagle, Tennessee, and marked the first time Rosa had ever been involved in an integrated learning environment. The training was going to be an encouragement for Mrs. Parks and would subsequently change her life and the lives of a nation forevermore.

On that fateful night of history, December 1, 1955, Rosa Parks had just completed her day's work at the Montgomery Fair department store as a tailor's assistant and was headed for the bus stop. Rosa was tired and gladly slid into the seat directly behind the white section to rest her weary body. Because of the segregation laws in Montgomery at the time, blacks were not allowed to sit in the front of the bus, even if there was no one else on board at the time. The bus drivers often instructed the African-American riders to enter at the door to the back of the bus so as to not walk past the white passengers. This night Rosa recognized the bus driver as the same one that ordered her off the bus some twelve years earlier to re-enter at the back door.

This driver had evicted her from the bus when she refused to re-enter as he had instructed her to do, even after she had paid her fare, which was the same as the white passengers.

Disturbingly, this bus driver was now demanding Rosa to relinquish her seat to white passengers that had just boarded. When she refused to give up her seat, the driver threatened to have her arrested immediately. Mrs. Parks remained seated right where she was, not only because she was physically tired from her day's work, but even more so because she was fed up with the treatment she and other African-Americans had been subjected to all of their lives. In her book, *Quiet Strength*, she wrote, "Our mistreatment was just not right, and I was tired of it. I kept thinking about my mother and my grandparents and how strong they were. I knew there was a possibility of being mistreated, but an opportunity was being given to me to do what I had asked of others."

When the bus pulled to a grinding halt, several policemen entered and removed Mrs. Parks, arresting her and taking her to police headquarters. This was certainly not the first time an African-American had been arrested for disobeying the segregation laws, but this time there was an important Supreme Court decision that tipped the scale of justice ever so slightly in their favor. An important decision had been rendered in Brown vs. Board of Education, which held that educational segregation was inherently illegal. With this major victory waving as a banner of encouragement, African-Americans were determined to fight more boldly for the end of racial segregation in every area of American life.

Because of Rosa's act of bravery, the NAACP officials and the Montgomery church leaders decided that Parks' arrest could provide the necessary catalyst for a successful bus boycott. African-American riders comprised 70 percent of the bus company's passengers, so they were asked to stop riding the buses until the company was willing to revise their illegal policies regarding them. Not only that, the NAACP and the church leaders asked that the bus company hire African-American bus drivers as well. This movement led to meetings at the Dexter Avenue Baptist Church, where the ministers and their congregations formed the Montgomery Improvement Association and elected the young Reverend Martin Luther King, Jr., as president. Their decisive action created exciting results, propelling the boycott of the buses to a successful 381 days. Eventually the case was taken to the Supreme Court, where the justices declared that segregation of the Montgomery buses was illegal and officially desegregated them on December 20, 1956.

Many of those involved were fired by their employers or continually harassed by angry whites who could not or would not accept the ruling by the Supreme Court. Rosa and some of her family had been fired and harassed as well, so in 1957 she and Raymond decided to move to Detroit, Michigan. It was extremely difficult for them to find work, but Parks was finally employed by Congressman John Conyers Jr., an African-American civil rights leader, to manage his Detroit office in 1965. Rosa worked for Congressman Conyers for twenty-five years while continuing her work with NAACP and the Southern Christian Leadership Conference (SCLC) and serving as the deaconess at the Saint Matthew African Methodist Episcopal Church.

Mrs. Parks received numerous awards, including an honorary degree form Shaw College in Detroit, the NAACP Spingarn Medal, and an annual Freedom Award presented in her honor by the SCLC. In 1980 she was awarded the Martin Luther King Jr. Nonviolent Peace Prize and in 1984 the Eleanor Roosevelt Women of Courage Award.

In 1988 she founded the Rosa and Raymond Parks Institute for Self-Development to train African-American youth for leadership roles, and she began serving as the institute's president. Rosa was in much demand as a public speaker and traveled extensively to share her role in the birth of the civil rights movement. She had spent a life giving of herself and dedicating her time to others, so in September 1994 when Rosa was beaten and robbed in her Detroit home, America was mortified to hear of this atrocious crime against her. She had lived through so many years of mistreatment to now have to endure such a heinous crime. Americans prayed and waited for God to restore Rosa. It is with gratitude to God that she was able to recover from this assault and move forward, always in grace and fortitude.

One of Rosa's many accolades came when her accomplishments were honored at the John F. Kennedy Center for the Performing Arts in Washington, D.C. In 1998 Parks was recognized with the first International Freedom Conductor Award given by the National Underground Railroad Freedom Center. Perhaps one of her highest and most cherished honors came in 1999 when President Bill Clinton awarded her the Congressional Gold Medal, the nation's highest civilian honor.

Rosa Parks met Pope John in the winter of 2000 in St. Louis, MO, and gave a statement to him asking for racial healing. She even received an award from the NAACP for Best Supporting Actress in the television series, *Touched By an Angel*, in which she appeared in the episode "Black Like Monica." Troy State University at Montgomery opened "The Rosa Parks Library and Museum" on the site where Mrs. Parks was arrested and the Montgomery bus boycott began 45 years before.

"The Rosa Parks Story" was filmed in Montgomery, Alabama, and shown on the CBS television network on February 24, 2002, and Mrs. Parks continued to receive numerous awards for the rest of her life. In fact it was as though America could not give her enough awards, enough accolades, enough love to show her how much we esteemed her for her courageous act of fidelity to the cause of ending racial segregation. We showered her with honors to try and say just how much we not only loved her, but how much we wished and hoped we could be like her if we were ever to confront evil the way she had on the night of December 1, 1955.

God was with Rosa Parks from the day she was born, through the nights of terror listening to the Klan ride under the cover of darkness, and on that fateful bus ride so many years ago. Our Savior Jesus Christ instilled courage in the heart of a little girl who was persecuted simply for being who God created her to be in this world. Her decision to act peacefully, lead with dignity and pray for her oppressors sparks a flame in us all. A flame that is fanned by her courage, a flame that will not die out as long as we breathe deeply of the freedom she fought so valiantly for and won.

Mrs. Rosa Parks, Matriarch of the civil rights movement, died on October 24, 2005 at the age of 92. She leaves a legacy of quiet courage, perseverance, dignity and grace to those who would hold her flame high, following her into the presence of Almighty God.

Scripture Application

GIVE HER THE REWARD
SHE HAS EARNED,
AND LET HER WORKS
BRING HER PRAISE
AT THE CITY GATE.

PROVERBS 31:31

AFRICAN FIRE LILY

ON A STARLESS NIGHT, ONE CAN SEE FLAMES LEAP FROM A FIELD SET AFIRE
IN A CONTROLLED BURN. THIS FLOWER IS ACTUALLY BROUGHT TO LIFE BY
HEAT AND FIRE. MUCH LIKE THE FIRE LILY, SOJOURNER TRUTH ROSE OUT
OF SMOLDERING ASHES TO HERALD A NEW LIFE CREATED BY GOD.

Sojourner Truth

1797–1883

Former Slave and
Champion for Human Rights

Sojourner Truth was born in 1797 in Hurley, New York, Ulster County, to James and Elizabeth, slaves of a wealthy man from Holland who lived in upstate New York. One of 13 children, Sojourner Truth was named Isabella Baumfree and spoke only Dutch until she was taken away from her family and sold. Young Isabella was very intelligent and learned to speak English quickly to help protect herself from her cruel, new master, but she continued to speak with a Dutch accent for the rest of her days.

Isabella was sold many times and when she was purchased by her third master, John Dumont, as a teenager, he married her to an older slave named Thomas. Isabella and Thomas had five children, and Dumont cruelly sold off several of their children. Heartbroken, she stayed on the Dumont farm until a few months before the state of New York ended slavery in 1828. Isabella stayed on the farm because Dumont had promised her freedom a year before the state emancipation. Instead she ran away with her infant son when he backed out of his earlier promise.

Favor was with Isabella when a kind, Quaker family, by the name of Van Wagener took both mother and child into their family. The Van Wageners even went so far as to help Isabella win a lawsuit against Dumont to have her son Peter returned to her care. Now Isabella was finally free and ready to strike out on her own.

Eventually settling in New York City, Isabella found work as a domestic for several religious communes, one known as the "Kingdom of Matthias." Isabella's mother had taught her about God and instructed her in the love of Jesus Christ, and the knowledge of this loving God had sustained her throughout her many troubles. In 1843, when the "religious" commune she worked for became involved in a scandal of adultery and murder Isabella became inspired by a spiritual revelation that would change her life forever. It was then that Isabella said that God told her to change her name to Sojourner Truth, and that is who she became from that moment forward.

Sojourner was an extremely tall woman, towering over most men of her time at a lofty 6 feet tall. Her presence was daunting and when she took to the road to spread the Gospel, people would stop and listen as she preached "God's truth and plan for salvation." Sojourner traveled great distances, walking through Long Island and Connecticut, and after months of travel she finally arrived in Northampton and joined the community known as "The Northampton Association for Education and Industry." There she met with such great abolitionists as William

Lloyd Garrison, Frederick Douglass and Olive Gilbert. Her dictated memoirs were published in 1850 as *The Narrative of Sojourner Truth: a Northern Slave*. Sojourner now added abolitionist to her growing oratory, often giving personal testimony about her life experiences as a slave and as a free woman through her Savior Jesus Christ.

During the Civil war, Sojourner traveled to Washington D.C. to sing and preach in an effort to earn money for the black soldiers in the Union army. After the war she decided to settle in Washington where she was able to continue to speak on the abolition of slavery. With her dedication and passion she actually attempted to persuade congress to donate free land in the west to former slaves.

Sojourner also became passionate about the women's suffrage movement. So along with her speeches on abolition and God's truth of salvation for mankind, she spoke out on women's rights. Her famous speech "Ain't I a Woman," delivered extemporaneously
at the Women's Convention in Akron, Ohio, in 1851, is one of power, courage and intelligence.

The speech was recorded by Frances Gage, feminist activist and one of the authors of the huge compendium of materials, *The History of Women's Suffrage*. Gage, who was presiding over the meeting, describes the event:

[*Author's note: The language used by those in attendance at this event is deemed racist and is exactly the reason we persist and pray so diligently, as Sojourner and others did, against prejudice and hate.*]

"The leaders of the movement trembled upon seeing a tall, gaunt black woman in a gray dress and white turban, surmounted with an uncouth sunbonnet march deliberately into the church, walk with the air of a queen up the aisle, and take her seat upon the pulpit steps. A buzz of disapprobation was heard all over the house, and there fell on the listening ear, "An abolition affair!" "Woman's rights and n-----s!" "I told you so!" "Go it, darkey!..." Again and again, timorous and trembling ones came to me and said, with earnestness, "Don't let her speak, Mrs. Gage, it will ruin us. Every newspaper in the land will have our cause mixed up with abolition and n-----s and we shall be utterly denounced." My only answer was, "We shall see when the time comes."

The second day the work waxed warm: Methodist, Baptist, Episcopal, Presbyterian, and Universalist ministers came in to hear and discuss the resolutions presented. One claimed superior rights and privileges for man, on the grounds of "superior intellect"; another, because of the "manhood of Christ," if God had desired the equality of woman, He would have given some token of His will through the birth, life and death of the Savior." Another gave us a theological view of the "sin of our first mother."

There were very few women in those days who dared to "speak in meeting," and the august teachers of the people were seemingly getting the better of us while the boys in the galleries, and the sneerers among the pew, were hugely enjoying the discomfiture, as they supposed, of the "strong-minded." Some of the tender-skinned friends were on the point of losing dignity and the atmosphere betokened a storm. When, slowly from her seat in the corner rose Sojourner Truth, who till now, had scarcely lifted her head. "Don't let her speak!" gasped half a dozen in my ear. She moved slowly and solemnly to the front, laid her old bonnet at her feet and turned her great speaking eyes to me. There was a hissing sound of disapprobation above and below. I rose and announced, "Sojourner Truth," and begged the audience to keep silence for a few moments.

The tumult subsided at once, and every eye was fixed on the almost Amazon form, which stood nearly six feet high, head erect and eyes piercing the upper air like one in a dream. At her first word there was a profound hush. She spoke in deep tones, which though not loud, reached every ear in the house, and away through the throng at the doors and windows.

The Speech
(in modern dialect)

Sojourner Truth, her first language being Dutch, spoke in a dialect that is perhaps difficult for the modern reader. The following is the speech rendered in a modern dialect:

Well, children, where there is so much racket there must be something out of kilter. I think that 'twixt the negroes of the South and the women at the North, all talking about rights, the white men will be in a fix pretty soon. But what's all this here talking about?

That man over there says that women need to be helped into carriages, and lifted over ditches, and to have the best place everywhere. Nobody ever helps me in to carriages, or over mud-puddles, or gives me any best place! And ain't I a woman? Look at me! Look at my arm! I have ploughed and planted, and gathered into barns, and no man could head me! And ain't I a woman? I could work as much and eat as much as a man—when I could get it—and bear the lash as well! And ain't I a woman? I have borne thirteen children, and seen most all sold off to slavery, and when I cried out with my mother's grief, none but Jesus heard me! And ain't I a woman?

Then they talk about this thing in the head; what's this they call it? [A member of the audience whispers, "intellect"] That's it honey. What's that got to do with women's rights or negroes' rights? If my cup won't hold but a pint, and yours holds a quart, wouldn't you be mean to let me have my little half measure full.

That little man in black there, he says women can't have as much rights as men, 'cause Christ wasn't a woman! Where did your Christ come from? Where did your Christ come from? From God and a woman! Man had nothing to do with Him.

If the first woman God ever made was strong enough to turn the world upside down all alone, these women together ought to be able to turn it back, and get it right side up again! And now they is asking to do it, the men better let them.

Obliged to you for hearing me, and now old Sojourner ain't got nothing more to say.

Amid roars of applause, she returned to her corner leaving more than one of us with streaming eyes and hearts beating with gratitude. She had taken us up in her strong arms and carried us safely over the slough of difficulty turning the whole tide in our favor. I have never in my life seen anything like the magical influence that subdued the mobbish spirit of the day, and turned the sneers and jeers of an excited crowd into notes of respect and admiration. Hundreds rushed up to shake hands with her and congratulate the glorious old mother and bid her God-speed on her mission of 'testifyin' agin concerning the wickedness of this 'ere people."

Sojourner Truth worked tirelessly all her life to help others know God's truth about all his children. Upon her death at the age of 86, I believe she left this unruly world a little bit brighter, wiser and filled with a hope not easily diminished nor extinguished. I also believe that Jesus welcomed his daughter home with these tender words, "Well done, my good and faithful servant, well done." Sojourner Truth, a truly great woman of courage, faith and grace.

Scripture Application

THERE IS NEITHER
JEW NOR GREEK,
SLAVE NOR FREE,
MALE NOR FEMALE,
FOR YOU ARE ALL ONE
IN CHRIST JESUS.

GALATIANS 3:28

SWEET WILLIAM
SOME MAY SAY THIS FLOWER IS FAR TOO BUSY AND FUSSY,
BUT HAVE YOU EVER SEEN THE FATHER'S GARDEN? THE MAGNIFICENT
DIVERSITY DISPLAYED THERE ENCOURAGES A CLOSER LOOK
TO APPRECIATE HIS HANDIWORK. IN HER UNIQUENESS,
JULIA WARD HOWE DISPLAYED COURAGE, FAITH AND DETERMINATION
THROUGH THE STRENGTH OF CHRIST.

Julia Ward Howe

1819 - 1910

"Battle Hymn of the Republic"

Julia Ward Howe was born into a life of privilege in New York City, the sixth child of Julia Rush Cutler and Samuel Ward. Her parents were both direct descendants of two colonial Rhode Island governors, Richard and Samuel Ward. Julia's life of ease included an exclusive education from attentive governesses, private schools and summers idly spent on Aquidneck Island at her families' cottage "Buttonwood," sometimes called "Redwood Lodge." Her mother oversaw the running of the household and would have been a protective buffer in life for her children had she not died when Julia was only five years old. Her father, Samuel, an Episcopalian and a strict Calvinist, was very protective of his brood, dominating every aspect of their young lives.

Samuel was a wealthy banker who could well afford the finest voice and music teachers for his precocious daughter Julia.

Their elegant home on Bond Street had an extensive library and art gallery where Julia spent a great deal of her time. She had learned French from early childhood, sharpened her skills in Italian, and at 14, added German and mastered the ability to read Latin and Greek with ease. At 16 she made the decision to leave school and, in her own words, "began thereafter to study in good earnest," continuing all of her life to study history, philosophy and literature. It was no surprise that at the age of 20 she had written literary criticism published anonymously in the *Literary and Theological Review* and the *New York Review*.

Julia enjoyed the fashionable social scene of her youth, becoming wildly popular due to her high spirits, auburn hair, blue eyes and beautiful voice. It didn't hurt much either that her brother, Samuel Ward, Jr., married into the very wealthy Astor family, who at the time were the epitome of social grace and stature.

It was the death of her father in 1839 and the soon after deaths of a brother and sister-in-law that moved Julia to turn to the religion of her upbringing, though her reading had exposed her to perhaps more liberal ideas than she had been taught. During her lifetime and into the present age there has been much controversy surrounding Julia because of her stance on women's rights and the right of women to be treated with dignity and respect. When we reflect on the words of her famous hymn, "Battle Hymn of the Republic," we see a woman who loved the Lord with all of her heart, mind and soul. Perhaps she will always be controversial, but I believe she was honest and open with her heavenly Father, praying all the while that women would eventually share in the fullness of life alongside men. It is only when man experiences the full love of Christ that he can embrace his wife with the same love that Jesus showers on His bride, the church.

Julia was an intelligent woman with many passionate views and ideas on a variety of issues that were the focal point of her world at the time. It was because of her rock solid position on these issues that she became attracted to a man that would be her future husband. While on a trip to Boston in 1841, she met Samuel Gridley Howe, noted philanthropist, educator, and founder of the Perkins Institute for the blind. Julia had visited the Institute through an invitation from her friends Henry Wadsworth Longfellow and Charles Sumner, and while there Howe rode up on his black horse. Julia later remembered it this way, "a noble rider on a noble steed." Samuel Gridley Howe was indeed a "noble" actually bearing the title "Chevalier of the Order of St. Savior" through his heroic acts during the Greek war for independence. Though eighteen years her senior they began a courtship and married in the spring of 1843, settling in Boston where the social circle shunned Julia because of her New York background.

It was her husband's desire to have a wife that would support him in his work, and he had great misgivings that his socialite wife would be up to the task at hand. Though they were both strongly attracted to one another they were aware that there could be problems ahead in their marriage. Samuel was serious and almost compulsively obsessed with his work; Julia was witty, brilliant, loved literature, music, and the social scene.

Just a week after marrying, the Howes sailed for Europe with Horace and Mary Mann, also recently married. If Julia had any expectations of a romantic honeymoon they were immediately quelled as they attended intensive tours of educational institutions instead of the quiet time together that she had imagined. A mere six weeks into their marriage and their European "vacation" she realized that she took a painful second place to her husband's work and close male friends. The following year Howe wrote to Sumner, "Julia says—Sumner ought to have been a woman and you to have married her: but...Julia is my love as a wife."

In Rome in 1844, their first child was born, christened by Theodore Parke—a friend who had come on a European trip and a frequent visitor to the couple's home in Boston. They would have five children in twelve years, a sixth born later died in early childhood.

The couple returned to Boston, eventually settling in a house that Julia named "Green Peace." They lived here between 1846 and 1864. Julia's faith was very important to her, and you could find her faithfully worshipping at the Channing Memorial Church where she relished her escape from isolation at home. It was her faith that helped her endure a stifling marriage that offered little in the way of respect or encouragement from her husband. Samuel Howe expected his wife to behave as a traditional wife and reminded her often that her lot in life was that of a "woman's place." Julia's ideas were neither valued nor accepted, and she felt the sting of the confinement of her marriage to Samuel.

Julia could no more be confined nor quieted than if an eagle be told not to soar to the heights of heaven. Her heart longed for the quiet days of youth in summers long ago, so in 1850 she acquired a summer residence in South Portsmouth at Lawton's Valley. Not far away, another property was purchased and became known as "Oak Glen," which became her long time summer home.

Julia wrote two anthologies of poems that were published in 1848, much to her husband's displeasure and her disquieted despair at his refusal to accept her writing.

However, while at Oak Glen in 1853 Julia was pleased to enjoy a rare opportunity to work with her husband when he edited *The Commonwealth,* a free-soil journal, and she contributed social and literary criticism. It was with great enthusiasm that she undertook helping her husband and only wished he would allow her more opportunity to share his interests and life. This was the only time that she had the brief chance to feel needed by Samuel and one can only surmise that this was one of her greatest disappointments in life.

Passion Flowers, a collection of Julia's poems was published anonymously in 1854, but the author's true identity soon became common knowledge. George Ripley of the *New York Tribune* called the poems "a product wrung with tears and prayer from the deepest soul of the writer…They form an entirely unique class in the whole range of female literature." Ednah Dow Cheney wrote that "it really is a grave thing, and, in this country, a rare thing, to publish such a book as this." Publisher George Ticknor received a letter from Hawthorne that said the book seemed "to let out a whole history of domestic unhappiness…"What does her husband think of it?"

"Chev was very angry about the book," Julia wrote to her sister, "and I really thought at one time that he would have driven me to insanity, so horribly did he behave." In her journal she wrote: "I have been married twenty years today. In the course of that time I have never known my husband to approve of any act of mine which I myself valued. Books-poems-essays-everything has been contemptible in his eyes because [it's] not his way of doing things…I am much grieved and disconcerted."

At one point they contemplated divorce, but Samuel's demand to keep two of the children ended the matter for Julia. She wrote to her sister that "his dream was to marry again—

some young girl who would love him supremely…I thought it my real duty to give up everything that was dear and sacred to me, rather than be forced to leave two of my children…I made the greatest sacrifice I can ever be called upon to make."

The troubled marriage continued, but adjustments were eventually made on both sides, though a lingering problem was Howe's management of Julia's inheritance. "His tyrannical instincts," she wrote, "more than any direct purpose, have made him illiberal with me in money matters, and if he can possibly place this so I cannot easily use it, he will, only because money is power, and a man never wishes a woman to have any which she does not derive from him."

Then in 1857, Julia's book of poems, *Words for the Hour*, came out as well as her play, *The World's Own*, which was performed in New York and Boston. In 1860 her report of a trip to Cuba was published in the *New York Tribune*. The article recounted a trip that she and Samuel took to accompany Theodore Parker on the first leg of his last journey to Italy where he died. Upon bidding Parker adieu in Havana, Julia wrote, they saw "between the slouched hat and the silver beard, the eyes that we can never forget, that seemed to drop back in the darkness with the solemnity of a last farewell."

Having grown up in a strict, Calvinist household with hellfire and damnation expounded at every turn, Julia longed for the promise of a tender and forgiving God and found this haven in James Freeman Clarke's Church of the Disciples. The informal nature of Clarke's Music Hall service did not exude the reverent, formal attitude that Samuel required for his children, but Julia thought Clarke "had not the philosophic and militant genius of Parker, but he had a genius of his own, poetical, harmonizing. In after years I esteemed myself fortunate to have passed from the drastic discipline of the one to the tender and reconciling ministry of the other." It was this acknowledgement of a loving, merciful God that ministered most to Julia's weary, beleaguered soul.

Julia's heart for justice caused her to have increased concerns for the Nation's ongoing battle over slavery. It was during the 1850s that Parker and Howe had drawn Julia into William Lloyd Garrison's anti-slavery group. Julia developed a deep respect and admiration for him and other abolitionist leaders including Wendell Phillips and Thomas Wentworth Higginson. Both Howes worked with the Sanitary Commission when war broke out and traveled to Washington D.C. to watch a Union army review that was suddenly dispersed by a Confederate attack. On the way back to the city in their carriage surrounded by retreating troops, the Howe party began to sing patriotic songs including the popular "John Brown's Body." James Freeman Clarke, one of the party, suggested to Julia that she write new and better lyrics for the tune.

During that night in her hotel, the words to "The Battle Hymn of the Republic" began to form in Julia's mind. She was careful to not wake the children and groped about in the dark for a stub of a pencil and paper to write the words to the hymn before they escaped into the night. In the morning she only made a few minor changes to the song. In February 1862, *The Atlantic* published "The Battle Hymn," paying its author $5. The song caught on gradually until it engulfed the North with its resounding words of victory.

This grand work is now America's national anthem for freedom and has been sung at the funerals of British statesman Winston Churchill, American senator Robert Kennedy, and American presidents Ronald Reagan and Richard Nixon. I still thrill at hearing the power of the hymn's words and feel the spirit soaring within me, carrying me on the winds of hope and truth. It is the song my grade school chorus sang during a quickly arranged assembly upon our hearing of President John F. Kennedy's assassination. My 11-year-old mind and heart leapt with patriotism, my eyes welling up in salty tears that stung and blurred my vision as they fell unashamedly down my flushed cheeks. This hymn has a way of touching and stirring the heart with the righteousness of Almighty God, a Just God, a Victorious and powerful God.

Julia appeared publicly many times during and after the war and in 1864 she read a poem at a gala event honoring William Cullen Bryant's 70th birthday. It also pleased her to read her essays and lectures to private gatherings, and she was elated upon being invited to join the Radical Club that was held at the homes of Cyrus Bartol and John T. Sargent. Other members were Ralph Waldo Emerson, Frederic Henry Hedge, Octavius Brooks Frothingham, Thomas Wentworth Higginson, William Henry Channing and James Freeman Clarke.

"It was a glad surprise to me," she wrote, "when I was first invited to read a paper before this august assemblage…I did indeed hear at these meetings much that pained and even irritated me." Howe had studied Comte, Hegel, Spinoza, Kant and Swedenborg and noted that "nothing of what I had heard or read had shaken my faith in the leadership of Christ in the religion which makes each man the brother of all, and God the beneficent father of each and all, the religion of humanity. Neither did this my conviction suffer any disturbance through the view presented by speakers at the Radical Club."

The importance of justice was foremost in Julia's mind and women's rights were always of the greatest importance to her. In 1868 Julia, with friend Lucy Stone and others, founded the New England Women's Club, which later became the American Women Suffrage Association. Howe lectured extensively on women's rights throughout the late 19th and early twentieth century. It was imperative to her that women would be liberated and be granted the right to vote and most importantly the right to be valued and heard. So in 1891 Julia founded the American Friends of Russian Freedom, and then serving as president of the United Friends of Armenia.

In 1871, Julia formed the Town and Country Club. Members included Samuel Coleman, Charlotte Chushman and George E. Waring. This diverse club included activities that revolved around a strong literary emphasis, as Julia was renowned for her literary abilities as an author, poet, hymn writer and orator. The club's members comprised a widely diverse populace, from a wide range of geographical and cultural backgrounds.

Julia once recalled that "During the first two thirds of my life, I looked to the masculine idea of character as the only true one, I sought its inspiration, and referred my merits and demerits to its judicial verdict...The new domain now made clear to me was that of true womanhood—woman no longer in her ancillary relation to her opposite, man, but in her direct relation to the divine plan and purpose, as a free agent, fully sharing with man every human right and every human responsibility. This discovery was like the addition of a new continent to the map of the world, or of a new testament to the old ordinances."

The change in Julia was noted by her friend Higginson wondering at her as she discovered this new domain: "It gave a new brightness to her face, a new cordiality in her manner, made her calmer, firmer; she found herself among new friends and could disregard old critics."

During the Franco-Prussian war of the 1870s Julia felt "the cruel and unnecessary character of the contest...a return to

barbarism, the issue having been one which might easily have
been settled without bloodshed." War was for the uncivilized
and heathen and she ventured out on a one-woman crusade
that began with an impassioned "appeal to womanhood: to
rise against war. She translated her proclamation into a variety
of languages and widely distributed them around the world.
Traveling to London she attempted to promote an international
Woman's Peace Congress but was not able to bring it to pass.

In 1873 and 1875, Julia Ward Howe traveled with her
husband to Santo Domingo and preached there several times
in a small Protestant church. Samuel's long held resistance to
his wife's public appearances had softened into an amused
admiration of her abilities. The most touching part of their many
years of marriage came before his death in 1876. He confessed
his marital transgressions to his wife and the tension between
them dissolved. When Julia's biography of her husband, *Memoir
of Dr. Samuel Gridley Howe*, was released in 1876 it was full of
praise for his character and great achievements.

Julia determined after Samuel died to begin a lecture tour
through the west to raise money for a two-year trip to Europe
and the Middle East with her youngest daughter Maud. While
visiting relatives in Italy, a niece described her Aunt Julia
at 60 as "a small woman of no particular shape or carriage,
clothes never quite taken care of, her bonnets never quite
straight on her head; and yet there was about her presence an
unforgettable distinction and importance. Her speaking voice
was very beautiful, and her face had a sensitive gravity, a look
of compassionate wisdom, until a twinkle of fun rippled over
it and a naughty imp laughed in her eyes."

Back in Boston, Julia continued writing and lecturing,
organizing women's clubs wherever she went. She even gave an

address in 1893 at the World Parliament of Religions in Chicago titled "What is Religion?"

Finally recognition and honor, long overdue, came to Julia Ward Howe in 1908 when she became the first woman elected to the American Academy of Arts and Letters. Not only did she garner this esteemed election, but three honorary doctorates of letters degrees as well. The citation from Smith College, best explains her importance: Poet and Patriot, lover of letters and learning; advocate for over half a century in print and living speech of great cause of human liberty; (and) sincere friend of all that makes for the elevation and enrichment of women. They even included "The Battle Hymn of the Republic" in the ceremony, often performed to celebrate her appearances.

When younger women sought her out in her last years and interviewed her, she always gave them motherly advice. With one such young woman she advised, "Study Greek, my dear, it's better than a diamond necklace." On her 91st birthday a reporter asked her for a motto for the women of America. She recommended, "Up to date!"

Julia died at her beloved summer home, Oak Glen, in the fall of 1910 under autumn skies and falling leaves. The funeral was held quietly in her church of many years, Church of the Disciples and at Symphony Hall with crowds overflowing both buildings. Maud Howe Elliott wrote, "A long succession of meetings of commemoration were held by her church, her clubs, the many associations she had founded and worked for. So great was the outpouring of love and reverence that it seemed [as if] her beloved name were writ in fire across the firmament."

Julia Ward Howe dedicated her life to justice for the oppressed in society—the God-given freedom that was being withheld from slave and womankind. Often controversial, often misunderstood, she truly was a distinctive woman who changed the world through her faith in God.

"Battle Hymn of the Republic"

Mine eyes have seen the glory of the coming of the Lord;
He is trampling out the vintage where the grapes of wrath
    are stored;
He hath loosed the fateful lightning of His terrible swift sword;
His truth is marching on.
Glory! Glory! Hallelujah! Glory! Glory! Hallelujah!
Glory! Glory! Hallelujah! His truth is marching on.

I have seen Him in the watch fires of a hundred circling camps
They have builded Him an altar in the evening dews and damps:
I can read His righteous sentence by the dim and flaring lamps;
His day is marching on.
Glory! Glory! Hallelujah! Glory! Glory! Hallelujah!
Glory! Glory! Hallelujah! His day is marching on.

I have read a fiery Gospel writ in burnished rows of steel;
"As ye deal with my contemners, so with you My grace shall deal";
Let the Hero, born of woman, crush the serpent with His heel,
Since God is marching on.
Glory! Glory! Hallelujah! Glory! Glory! Hallelujah!
Glory! Glory! Hallelujah! Since God is marching on.

He has sounded forth the trumpet that shall never call retreat;
He is sifting out the hearts of men before His judgment seat;
Oh be swift, my soul, to answer Him! Be jubilant, my feet;
Our God is marching on.
Glory! Glory! Hallelujah! Glory! Glory! Hallelujah!
Glory! Glory! Hallelujah! Our God is marching on.

In the beauty of the lilies Christ was born across the sea,
With a glory in His bosom that transfigures you and me:
As He died to make men holy, let us live to make men free;
[originally, let us die to make men free]
While God is marching on.
Glory! Glory! Hallelujah! Glory! Glory! Hallelujah!
Glory! Glory! Hallelujah! While God is marching on.

He is coming like the glory of the morning on the wave,
He is wisdom to the mighty, He is honor to the brave;
So the world shall be His footstool, and the soul of wrong His slave,
Our God is marching on.
Glory! Glory! Hallelujah! Glory! Glory! Hallelujah!
Glory! Glory! Hallelujah! Our God is marching on.

Scripture Application

> I KNOW THAT THE LORD
> SECURES JUSTICE FOR THE POOR AND
> UPHOLDS THE CAUSE OF THE NEEDY.
> SURELY THE RIGHTEOUS WILL
> PRAISE YOUR NAME AND THE
> UPRIGHT WILL LIVE BEFORE YOU.
>
> PSALM 140:12-13

ENGLISH ROSE
THE MERE PRESENCE OF THIS FLOWER IN THE GARDEN MAKES A
PEACEFUL, LOVING STATEMENT, HOLDING ITS OWN IN A REVERENT BOW
BEFORE THE KING OF KINGS AND LORD OF LORDS.
IT WAS AMY CARMICHAEL'S DEVOTED SPIRIT THAT SAVED A
MULTITUDE OF GIRLS FROM A LIFE OF DESPAIR AND SUFFERING.

Amy Carmichael

1867–1951

Missionary to India

The small village of Millisle in Northern Ireland was the humble birth place of Amy Beatrice Carmichael, the eldest of seven children born to devout Presbyterian parents.

Little Amy possessed an indomitable spirit in spite of being beset with illness for the better part of her childhood, suffering from neuralgia, a nerve disorder, which kept her confined to bed for weeks at a time. This disease process caused her whole body to become weak and achy, which prevented her from enjoying many family outings and gatherings. In spite of her illness, Amy loved to rough and tumble with her brothers and was somewhat of a tomboy, much to her father's delight. Perhaps he enjoyed seeing his young daughter having fun when he knew she was laid up so much of the time with her illness. She was always determined not to let anything stand in her way of doing what she wanted. But with her illness, it did seem very unlikely that young Amy would ever grow up to be able to do much of anything, let alone become a passionate missionary for Christ.

As a child Amy often dreamed of having beautiful blue eyes rather than her brown eyes, which she considered dull and plain. She even entreated her mother whether God would give her blue eyes if she wanted them and if she prayed hard enough. Her dear mother, Catherine, was a wise, God-fearing woman and she told her daughter, "Our Father in heaven always hears our prayers and wants to give us good things." With that bit of information Amy prayed that night to God that she might wake up in the morning with bright, blue eyes. When she leapt out of bed the next morning to view her image in the mirror, she was disappointed that God hadn't changed her brown eyes to the much prayed over set of blue ones.

It was not until Amy was an adult that she realized God's unique plan for her brown eyes, a divine plan that enabled her to reach out to the villagers she had been called to in India. Amy finally realized that if she had been born with the blue eyes she had wished for as a child, she would have had great difficulty gaining the Indians' trust. Amy treasured this knowledge in her heart and knew why she had brown eyes. God intended to use this trait to reach the Indian villagers with the good news of Jesus Christ. She knew without a doubt that God never makes mistakes.

Amy received a prompting from God as a young girl that gave her a glimpse of her work of compassion many years later. As she recounts the story in her writings, this prompting from God came on a blustery, winter's day as she and her brothers were returning home from a morning at church. Amy and her brothers noticed a feeble, old woman struggling along the road with a very large bundle. They felt compelled to reach out and help, but at the same time felt embarrassed to be seen helping because "this meant facing all the respectable people who were, like ourselves, on their way home. It was a horrid moment. We were only two boys and a girl, and not at all exalted Christians. We hated doing it. Crimson all over (at least we felt crimson, soul and body of us) we plodded on, a wet wind blows in about us, and blowing, too, the rags of that poor old woman, till she seemed like a bundle of feathers and we unhappily mixed up with them."

As they passed a beautiful Victorian fountain she heard the words of I Corinthians 3:12-14 in her spirit: "Gold, silver, precious stones, wood, hay, stubble—every man's work shall be made manifest: for the day shall declare it, because it shall be declared by fire; and the fire shall try every man's work of what sort it is. If any man's work abide." Startled, Amy turned to see who might have spoken these words to her, but no one was there, just the sound of the steady gurgle of water from the fountain and the laughter from people walking by. Perhaps she thought, just perhaps God was calling her away from her preoccupation with her social life and that it was now time to "settle some things with Him."

God was calling Amy to service in a way she soon was to discover when she and her family traveled to Glasgow, Scotland, in order to attend The Holiness Conference in Keswick, in England's Lake District. It was the fall of 1886 and the purpose of the conference was to promote "a higher calling of the Christian life." It was there that Amy felt God's hand on her life. "The hall was full of a sort of gray mist, very dull and chilly. I came to that meeting half hoping, half fearing. Would there be anything for me? ...The fog in the hall seemed to soak into me. My soul was in a fog. Then the chairman rose for the last prayer... 'O Lord, we know thou art able to keep us from falling.' Those words found me. It was as if they were a light. And they shone for me."

In that gray misty hall Amy realized that God was calling her to become "dead to the world and its applause, to all its customs, fashions, and laws." Nothing could be more important than living her life for Jesus Christ who, with nothing of worldly possessions, had given His life for her. She knew without a doubt that He was calling her to do the same and give her all to Him.

Amy's beloved father passed away, and she treasured her relationship with her mother, but when a family friend, Dr. Robert Wilson, asked if Amy might come and live with him and his two sons, her mother agreed to the request. Dr. Wilson had lost his only daughter to an illness and he wished to adopt Amy and become her mentor. Dr. Wilson was also co-founder of Keswick Convention and was able to tutor Amy for many years, giving her the gift of an abiding love for the teaching and ministering of the Scriptures.

Amy's heart was to serve her Lord wherever He wanted her to go, so initially she served for 15 months in Japan, but soon found her calling in India. Through the Church of England, Zenana Missionary Society, she was commissioned to go to Dohnavur, India. This place would become Amy's world and her lifelong vocation. She served faithfully there without furlough for 56 years.

The needs of all the people were desperate and intense, but even more so for the little children. Amy's heart went out to them and she founded the Dohnavur Fellowship that served as a sanctuary and refuge for more than one thousand children. Many of these children had been dedicated as temple prostitutes by their own parents. Through Amy's loving guidance these children found love and hope through Jesus Christ. To them she was "Amma," which means mother in the Tamil language. Her life was full of danger and stress, but she never forgot God's promise to "keep them in all things." The children were safe and that is what mattered most to Amy.

Her thoughts flitted back to when she was that little girl who so desperately wanted blue eyes, but as she noted once again, "God never makes mistakes." With her skin dyed brown with coffee, and her Indian dress, blue eyes would never have fit in with the people. All the workers at the Dohnaver Fellowship wore Indian dress to blend in with respect to the culture and all the children were given Indian names. Amy would walk great distances along the hot, dusty roads to save just one child from suffering.

"There were days when the sky turned black for me because of what I heard and knew was true ...Sometimes it was as if I saw the Lord Jesus Christ kneeling alone, as He knelt long ago under the olive trees...And the only thing that one who cared could do, was to go softly and kneel down beside Him, so that He would not be alone in His sorrow over the little children."

Sadly, Amy suffered a tragic accident in 1931 when she was badly injured in a fall, requiring her to spend much of her time in bed for the remainder of her life. Amy Carmichael died in India in 1951 at the age of 83. She asked that no stone be put over her grave; instead the children she had cared for put a bird bath over it with the single inscription "Amma," which means mother in the Tamil.

Amy Beatrice Carmichael, with brown eyes and compassionate heart, poured out her life to the children of India because Her Lord Jesus asked her to serve. Amy's response was

"Yes, Lord, here am I." Perhaps God is calling you to serve, maybe not in some far away place, but perhaps right in your own town, city, workplace, or school. Our Father in heaven can use you to make a difference in the lives of those who are lost and in need of hope.

A young woman once wrote Amy a letter explaining that she was considering life as a missionary and asked, "What is missionary life like?" Amy wrote back saying simply, "Missionary life is simply a chance to die."

Scripture Application

I WANT TO KNOW CHRIST
AND THE POWER OF HIS
RESURRECTION
AND THE FELLOWSHIP OF
SHARING IN HIS SUFFERINGS,
BECOMING LIKE HIM IN HIS
DEATH, AND SO, SOMEHOW, TO
ATTAIN TO THE RESURRECTION
FROM THE DEAD.

PHILIPPIANS 3:10

YELLOW ROSE
NOT RED, NOT PINK, BUT YELLOW—A YELLOW ROSE STANDS UNIQUE,
SAYING, "SEE WHAT GOD HATH BROUGHT FORTH TO
CONFOUND THE EYES AND STIR THE HEARTS OF MANKIND."
MARIAN ANDERSON PERSONIFIED THIS STATEMENT BY HER
ELOQUENT VOICE, GRACE AND HEART FOR HER SAVIOR.

Marian Anderson

1897–1993

Opera Star Who Persevered

On February 27, 1897, Marian Anderson was born the oldest of three children in Philadelphia. Her father died when she was a child and her mother took in laundry to support the family. The little girl began singing at 3 years of age and when she was 6 she joined the choir at the Union Baptist Church. She impressed the director by memorizing all the parts—soprano, alto, tenor and bass in all the hymns they sang during services. It wasn't until she was 15 that she began taking formal lessons, studying with Mary S. Patterson. To help offset the cost of her lessons, her church choir held fundraisers on her behalf. As she progressed to further, advanced studies with Agnes Reifsnyder and Giuseppe Boghetti, the Philadelphia Choral Society, a black ensemble, gave a benefit performance to support her as well.

Marian made her signature debut at the New York Philharmonic on August 27, 1925 when her teacher, Guiseppe Boghetti, entered her in a voice competition. The competition drew over 300 singers, and Boghetti was ecstatic when his pupil won first prize. A concert manager immediately signed her for several engagements, but after a few concerts, her engagements were far and few between. With few prospects for concerts in America, Marian decided to travel to Europe, not only in hopes of performing, but devoting herself as well to the opportunity to study the art of German lieder singing.

The time in Europe also presented many situations for her to perfect her command of many languages and secure many successful concerts. While in Scandinavia in 1930, she met the composer Jean Sibelius, who spoke glowingly of her voice and dedicated the song "Solitude" to her. Arturo Toscanini could not believe the beauty of her voice and was overheard saying to her, "A voice like yours can only be heard once in a hundred years." The impresario Sol Hurok offered to present her in another Town Hall recital upon hearing her sing in Paris that same year. Marian had many misgivings about the much more enthusiastic reception she received in Europe compared to the cool response she received in America. But Mr. Hurok was very persuasive and from that point on she was to benefit from his skills as her manager for the rest of her life.

Sol Hurok was right about the success of the Town Hall concert that was held on Dec. 30, 1935, "Let it be said from the Outset," Howard Taubnam wrote in the *Times*, "Marian Anderson has returned to her native land [as] one of the great singers of our time."

The demand to hear this "new" great voice of the twentieth century provided Miss Anderson with over 70 recitals a year in the United States. Unfortunately racial prejudice still prevailed in many instances. One such unfortunate display actually helped Marian become a household name and furthered the cause of equality in America. In 1939, Hurok attempted to book her at Constitution Hall in the national headquarters of the D.A.R. (Daughters of the American Revolution) and was promptly told that all dates were taken.

Perplexed, Sol Hurok pleaded his case to the public, and America's First Lady, Eleanor Roosevelt, resigned from the D.A.R. Other prominent women followed suit. When the Secretary of the Interior, Harold L. Ickes, extended the Lincoln Memorial to Miss Anderson for a concert on Easter Sunday, some 75,000 people arrived, with millions more listening in rapt attention to the radio broadcast. Photographs and films of Miss Anderson singing in front of the Lincoln Memorial statue quickly became a poignant symbol for the fledgling civil rights movement.

On a personal note, I have an interesting story about a visit Marian Anderson made to the Montana State Legislature in the 1940s. My paternal grandfather, Volney Andersen, was a member of the House of Representatives when she came to Montana for a series of concerts. As Miss Anderson entered the floor of the House of Representatives, all of the members stood in honor of their guest, except for a few who refused to stand and acknowledge her presence. When she sang, her voice reverberated throughout the Capitol building as her listeners sat spellbound by her performance. When she closed her rendition, the thunderous applause was deafening as the members leapt to their feet in heartfelt admiration, all except for the few legislators that could not find the decency to pay tribute to a truly great woman. I am proud to say that my dear grandfather was among those that respectfully stood to honor this grand woman of such great talent and grace.

Miss Anderson always maintained a quiet dignity for which she was famous, and declined to comment or to express any ill will towards those that behaved in disrespectful or prejudicial ways. No matter how hard the reporters pressed her she simply nodded and smiled, later writing in her memoir, "My Lord, What a Morning. I particularly did not want to say anything about the D.A.R. As I have made clear, I did not feel that I was designed for hand-to-hand combat."

When four years later, Miss Anderson was invited to sing at Constitution Hall by the D.A.R. for a China Relief concert, she said, "When I finally walked onto the stage of Constitution Hall, I felt no different than I had in other halls. There was no sense of triumph. I felt that it was a beautiful concert hall and I was very happy to sing there."

Looking back on her very lengthy career it is sad to note that the world of opera was never open to her, being denied until Rudolf Bing invited her to sing at the Met on January 7, 1955, but this was at the very end of her career. She became the first African-American singer to perform there—an amazing achievement, even though it was somewhat belated. Marian sang Ulrica in Verdi's *Ballo in Maschera*, and when the curtain rose on the second scene later that evening, she trembled when the audience applauded and applauded before she could sing a single note. Because of the opera houses being closed to her she continued her recital concerts, conveying a great power of communication with her closed eyes and very few gestures. She was the epitome of serene tranquility and dignified grace, her manner one of refined stateliness.

In 1957 Marian embarked on a ten-week tour of India and the Far East where she sang 24 concerts in 14 countries. To know that this was sponsored by the State Department helps to understand the value our nation's leadership placed on her ability to reach our allies on the world stage. Her presence in the American home grew in stature as well when this tour was filmed by a CBS New crew for a program entitled "The Lady From Philadelphia," to be used on the Edward R. Murrow series "See It Now." Perhaps the interest became so great at this time of her life due to the fact that people began to fully recognize the true greatness and gift of her vocal ability.

One of her greatest honors came early in 1957 when she sang at newly elected President Dwight D. Eisenhower's Inauguration. Then in 1961 she once again sang at an inauguration, this time for our handsome new President, John F. Kennedy. Later that year, 64-year-old Marian traveled to Berlin to perform for American troops, giving her all to them, even though she had passed her vocal prime. Having never toured Australia, she determined to sing there, and in 1962 she sang her heart out there as she began to think about the possibility of retiring from the arduous task of touring. It was in October of 1964 that she began her farewell tour at Constitution Hall, the same Hall that had previously refused her admittance for a concert. Miss Anderson performed her final recital at Carnegie Hall on April 18, 1965, and made occasional stage appearances in the 1970s as the reader for Aaron Copeland's *Lincoln Portrait*.

Our nation honored Miss Anderson in a variety of ways, from receiving the Medal of Freedom in 1963, to being among the first group to receive the Kennedy Center Honors in 1978. A half-ounce gold commemorative medal of her likeness was coined by the United States Treasury Department in 1980. In 1984 she was the recipient of the Eleanor Roosevelt Human Rights Award of the City of New York. President Ronald Reagan awarded her the National Arts Medal in 1986, adding honor upon honor to her lifetime of engaging the world through song.

Marian Anderson served her country in other ways, besides singing. President Eisenhower appointed her an alternative representative in the United States delegation to the Human Rights Committee of the United Nations. Whenever she could use her gift as a songstress to benefit social causes that meant a lot to her, she never hesitated. She sang again at the Lincoln Memorial in 1963 during the March on Washington for Jobs and Freedom, and gave benefit concerts for the National Association for the Advancement of Colored People, Congress of Racial Equality, and the America-Israel Cultural Foundation.

Marian found a kindred spirit in Orpheus H. Fisher, an architect, whom she married in 1943. He died in 1986. They had no children of their own, but Marian had a heart for young singers and made every effort to give aid to those with great promise. Upon becoming the recipient of the Philadelphia Bok prize in 1943, she promptly took the $10,000 she was awarded and established the Marian Anderson Award. This fund eventually ran out but was re-established in 1990 and annually awards prizes of $25,000. Miss Anderson was also involved with the Young Audiences Organization that utilizes professional musicians to perform concerts in our nation's schools. It was always her intention to serve directly with young people, encouraging them to strive for excellence. Of course, she was without a doubt, a huge role model and inspiration for young, black musicians who followed in her footsteps.

Miss Anderson sang all the classics and standard concert works, from Bach and Handel oratorio selections to Schubert, Brahms, Schumann and Rachmaninoff songs, to Verdi arias and spirituals. Her beautiful renderings of all of these works, especially Schubert's "Ave Maria," were much loved. However, it truly was her achievement in insisting that the spirituals deserved a place in the active repertory, and she made them the centerpieces of many programs. Spirituals such as "My Lord, What a Morning" and

"Crucifixion" were described by her this way: "They are my own music, but it is not why I love to sing them. I love them because they are truly spiritual in quality; they give forth the aura of faith, simplicity, humility and hope."

During her remaining years Marian spent most of her time at her Danbury, Connecticut, farm, which she named Marianna. During these final years she could occasionally be seen at concerts in New York City, even though she was now confined to a wheelchair. When she could no longer live alone she moved to Portland, Oregon, to live with her nephew, Mr. DePreist, who is her only survivor.

Marian Anderson was the embodiment of spiritual grace and dignity, a heart born out of determination and faith, strengthened through the love of Christ her savior. Valiantly she faced hate, disrespect and ignorance, all the while creating beauty in the world through her incredible voice.

Scripture Application

SHE IS CLOTHED WITH
STRENGTH AND DIGNITY;
SHE CAN LAUGH AT THE
DAYS TO COME.

PROVERBS 31:25

FLOWERS OF THE DOVE TREE
REST HERE, TARRY A WHILE BENEATH THE FRAGRANT BRANCHES AND
BREATH DEEP OF THE PEACE FOUND THERE. THE SHADE WILL PROVIDE
RELIEF AND GIVE YOU STRENGTH FOR THE REST OF THE JOURNEY.
THIS FLOWERING TREE REPRESENTS PANDITA RAMBAI'S LIFE, OFFERED TO
THOSE WHO SUFFERED AND NEEDED GOD'S ABUNDANT MERCY.

Pandita Rambai

1858-1922

Founder of School for Child-Widows in India

The idea of becoming a bride while still a child strikes most of the western world as apprehensible and unimaginable. But this practice was and still is the custom in many parts of India where Pandita Rambai was born.

Pandita was fortunate to have been born to a father who was an advocate for the education of women, a belief entirely contrary to Hindu beliefs. Pandita's father was a pundit, meaning teacher, and was very knowledgeable in the Hindu Shastras, instructing his little daughter so well, in fact, that she memorized 2,300 verses. So great was her father's love of teaching and his belief that all women should be permitted to learn, that he taught his wife as well, causing further outcry from his peers. Because of these views the family had to seek refuge by retreating to the jungles to make their home, away from those who sought them harm because of their beliefs. Most of Pandita's education occurred in the jungles of India and her aptitude and love of learning knew no bounds.

The family struggled in the jungles, but their commitment to embracing knowledge was very important to all of them, so they strove to survive amidst great difficulties. When Pandita was just sixteen years of age, famine struck the land and for a tortuous eleven days they subsisted on water and leaves. Because of this situation they were forced to leave the jungle and her father became an itinerant teacher for a number of years as a way to eke out a meager living for his family. When Pandita's mother and father died, she only had a brother to care for her and to look out for her well-being.

Because of her father's instruction and compassion towards his fellow man, Pandita's concern for the custom of child marriages encouraged her to become a lecturer repudiating this practice. She also became very outspoken about the education of women, her teachings attracting a great amount of attention from the punditi, or learned men in Calcutta. They summoned Rambai to appear before them, and after a lengthy examination, she passed with flying colors and received the title of *Sarasvati.*

Panditi had garnered quite a following and was experiencing much success from her lectures, but at the height of all her popularity, her brother died. Being left alone as a woman without a male relative placed Rambai in a precarious situation that was just not acceptable in Indian culture. This matter was resolved within six months when she married an educated Bengali man from a lower caste system. This detail was overlooked by Pandita and her new husband because they both had abandoned their Hindu beliefs.

Having settled into married life with a new baby daughter, Pandita believed that life was going well for her little family. However, after only nineteen months of marriage, her husband died. Left with her baby girl to care for, life looked rather bleak. She was a widow with a daughter and no son, so things could not have been worse. This situation was despised in India and because she had broken caste by marrying beneath her, she was shunned by all her relatives. The only thing left for the resilient Rambai was to face the world alone and begin lecturing again. Because of this turn of events, after a time she left her homeland and went to England.

Pandita had recently become a Christian and just as she had thrown herself into memorizing the verses of the Hindu Shastras as a girl, she studied the Bible with the same great love for the adventure of learning.

First studying the Bible in her native Sanskrit, she then tackled the scriptures in the English language, challenging herself to absorb this difficult language. Having worked diligently over time to perfect her English, she became a professor of Sanskrit in the Ladies College at Cheltenham.

Through all of her amazing accomplishments and many accolades, one would have thought Pandita would be relatively happy, but she just could not shake the images of the child-widows of India. Her heart could not escape the desperate situation these young girls faced in her native land, and she knew she would never be content as long as the children were suffering.

It was during her professorship that she was invited to America to attend the graduation of her cousin Joshee from a medical school in Philadelphia. Upon seeing the university, Rambai began to see great possibilities for education in her country. She began to study the American public school system, believing with all her heart that she could apply these same principals in India.

With much determination and purpose, Pandita completed her training with plans to return to India with the sole resolve to educate high-caste Hindu widows. Who better to educate and inspire than the woman who had suffered at the hands of the Hindu culture? This same culture brought many of the child-widows into shame and near death through starvation. In times of famine the custom was to turn the child-widows out to die or perhaps even worse, to be picked up by unsavory men who would use them and lead them into a life of utter degradation and humiliation.

Pandita was determined to rescue these castoffs and provide them with a life of hope and promise. Through her school that was opened in 1898, she taught 350 Child-widows to be able to enter their world enabled to not only survive, but to help others as well. In her first graduating class, she had fourteen that had been trained as teachers, seven as missionary assistants, and ten had homes of their very own.

Because of Pandita's heart for social justice and her love for her Savior Jesus Christ, lives were changed and tragedies averted. She knew that even if one soul was saved or one life changed for the better, all her hard work and determination was worth going through. In her school-home, these Hindu child-widows learned through Pandita's loving guidance how to become resilient and to know a life filled with hope through the love of Jesus Christ.

Your heart is your "home." Won't you open your "home" to those who may need the love of the Savior of the world? Won't you see the needs of the dispossessed and the unloved in the world around you, and invite them into your sphere of influence for a time of respite and renewal? Your heart will soar with the joy of helping someone who may be lonely or perhaps even despised.

And for you who have been a cast off and perhaps unloved, if you do not know the love of Jesus Christ, I invite you now to come to know Him personally. Repent (turn) from your sinful ways and ask Him into your heart and life. He will come and give you all the grace, peace and mercy you will need to live a fulfilled life. Jesus promises life eternal if you would just believe in Him. God bless you on this life-changing decision. (John 3:16)

Scripture Application

THEY SAID, "RABBI,
WHERE ARE YOU STAYING?"
"COME," HE REPLIED,
"AND YOU WILL SEE."

JOHN 1:38-39

"...WE WILL COME TO HIM AND
MAKE OUR HOME WITH HIM."

JOHN 14:23

GLORIOSA

THE GLORIOSA RESEMBLES FLAMES LEAPING TO TOUCH THE HEAVENS
WITH DETERMINATION AND CONFIDENCE IN THE CREATOR WHO
LOVINGLY DESIGNED IT. EVER-VIBRANT, MAHALIA JACKSON PROCLAIMED
GOD'S LOVE THROUGH HER SINGING, REASSURING THE WORLD THAT
THOUGH THE FLAMES OF LIFE CONSUME US, OUR SAVIOR JESUS CHRIST
LEADS US THROUGH TO SAFETY.

Mahalia Jackson

1911–1872

Gospel Singer & Civil Rights Champion

It was in the city rooted in soulful, spiritual music that Mahalia Jackson entered the world. Born the third child to parents Charity Clark and John A. Jackson in New Orleans, she faced an uncertain future at a very young age. Her father worked in the community as a barber and preacher, but when her mother, Charity, died in 1916 he sent 4-year-old Mahalia to live with her Aunt Mahalia "Duke" Paul.

Aunt Duke was a woman of strong Christian faith who quickly immersed her niece in her church, the Plymouth Rock Baptist Church in New Orleans. The 4-year-old Mahalia began singing in the choir that blended the freedom and power of the Gospel with the stricter style of the Baptist Church. Even at this young age she had a booming voice and would sing hymns and old-time Gospel tunes around the house. Aunt Duke never allowed secular music in her home, but as a teenager Mahalia's cousin would sneak in records that were an influence on her—singers like Bessie Smith, Enrico Caruso and Ma Rainey. Soon Mahalia's own style emerged into a more soulful expression that would be her signature sound throughout her life in music.

Deciding at the age of 16 to move to Chicago to work as a domestic, Mahalia soon found alternative work as a soloist at churches and funerals. Through her church, the Greater Salem Baptist Church, her reputation in the choir caught the attention of many small churches from coast to coast. Her unique contralto voice garnered a great deal of attention. However, the larger, more formal churches disapproved of her more energetic application of familiar hymns.

Mahalia began singing with a troop called the Prince Johnson Singers, and with high hopes she successfully signed to record as a soloist for Decca Records in 1937. She was very disappointed when her records did not sell as well as the recording studio had envisioned. In order to make a living, she turned to work as a beautician to support herself, while not totally giving up on her singing and her hope to work as an artist. Mahalia began touring with Thomas A. Dorsey at Gospel tents and churches, and as her following grew she was once again offered a recording contract with Apollo Records from 1946 to 1954. Then from 1954 to 1967 she made the switch to Columbia Records where she attained her greatest recognition as a spiritual and Gospel singer.

America's mainstream embraced Mahalia, and through the 1950s her booming voice could be heard on radio, television and concert halls around the world. When traveling in Europe on tour, she sang in concert halls packed with avid Gospel fans. In 1957 at the Newport Jazz Festival she held a special all-Gospel program that she had requested and her audience was enthusiastic, to say the least, by her passionate renditions of well-known Gospel hymns. It was through hosting her own Sunday night radio program in 1954 that really she began a stir of interest in her style of singing. And when Ed Sullivan invited her to perform on his program in 1956, she catapulted Gospel music into the American mainstream.

Mahalia Jackson fought against racial prejudices all of her life. When she sang for President Dwight Eisenhower and then for President John F. Kennedy's inaugural ball in 1960, she gave hope to the growing civil rights movement that change was on the horizon. It was because of her involvement in the civil right's movement that her voice became known as the sound of hope for equality.

The highlight of her involvement in the movement came when she sang an old slave spiritual before Dr. Martin Luther King, Jr.'s famous "I Have a Dream" speech at the March on Washington in 1963. She had performed many times at Dr. King's rallies, becoming very close with the civil rights leader and his family. Sadly, just five years later she sang at his funeral after our nation lost this great man.

In later years her doctors ordered her to slow down, but she would have none of that and subsequently collapsed while on stage in Munich in 1971. Because of her heart condition, she was relegated to her home in Evergreen, Illinois. She died from heart failure at home on January 27, 1972.

Mahalia Jackson had lived out the American dream, using her God-given gifts and talents to not only better her life, but elevate the lives of others with the Gospel message through her songs. She lived a life of sacrifice and service, truly as a woman of courage and faith.

Scripture Application

I WILL GIVE THANKS
TO THE LORD BECAUSE
OF HIS RIGHTEOUSNESS
AND WILL SING PRAISE
TO THE NAME OF THE
LORD MOST HIGH.

PSALM 7:17

PART TWO

Courage

for the

Great

Commission

YET WHEN I
PREACH THE GOSPEL,
I CANNOT BOAST,
FOR I AM COMPELLED
TO PREACH.
WOE TO ME
IF I DO NOT
PREACH THE GOSPEL.

DEUTERONOMY 31:6

Introduction to
Part Two

Courage for
The Great Commission

Those who minister the Gospel of Christ often feel that unless they are able to witness to the lost, they would not be able to contain the passion that wells up in their hearts. Just as the Apostle Paul exclaimed in I Corinthians 9:16, *"Yet when I preach the Gospel, I cannot boast, for I am compelled to preach. Woe to me if I do not preach the Gospel."*

The Holy Spirit impresses urgency on our hearts and minds to share the Good News of Jesus Christ with those who are lost and without hope. To preach to those who are the walking dead is a privilege that the body of Christ shares. No matter what your position or station in life might be, whether you are a secretary, a toll booth operator or a corporate CEO, if you belong to Christ you are compelled to share the hope of eternal life that our Lord offers through His death and resurrection.

As soon as Jesus ascended into heaven to sit at the right hand of the Father the great commission began in earnest. It was for truth and righteousness that the Apostles set forth to fulfill what their Lord had commanded of them. It was a calling that could only be heeded. To turn away would have been misery. They were all compelled to preach the Gospel and bring the lost into the kingdom of God.

The women of faith in the following stories were ordinary women who lived their faith in mighty ways, often facing dangers and horrible trials. They relied on Jesus, rested in Him, and stepped out into the unknown to capture the hearts of those who were in danger of spending eternity without God. Proclaiming the liberation of our Lord was as natural as breathing the air around them. All of these mighty women of God have since slipped from this life into the realm of heaven where we can now rest assured that they are, at this very moment, singing praises to God. May the Holy Spirit ignite the flame in your heart and mind to embrace courage and reach the lost for the kingdom of God.

FIELD OF POPPIES

NOT JUST ONE FLOWER, BUT A FIELD OF FLOWERS CASTING ITS CAPE BEFORE ALMIGHTY GOD IN A DISPLAY OF LOVE AND AFFECTION. AIMEE SEMPLE MACPHERSON LIVED HER LIFE IN JUST THIS WAY, TOUCHING MULTITUDES WITH THE LOVE OF JESUS CHRIST. HER COURAGE AND DETERMINATION IS AN ENCOURAGEMENT FOR WOMEN EVERYWHERE.

Aimee Semple McPherson

1890–1936

Evangelist, Writer and Founder of the Foursquare Church

On October 9, 1890, a tiny baby girl was born in the upstairs room of a farmhouse in Salford, Michigan, to proud parents, James and Minnie Kennedy.

James and Minnie were married in Michigan, across the border from their native Canada, after their May-December marriage drew cries of outrage from their small community. James was 50 years old and Minnie was only 14 years of age at the time. Their unlikely relationship came out of a very sad situation concerning James' first wife Elizabeth.

James Morgan Kennedy had been regularly caring for his wife Elizabeth as she struggled between life and death. Caring for Elizabeth became increasingly difficult and James knew he would have to find 24-hour nursing care to help with his dear wife. As she lay dying, he penned an advertisement for the local paper, pressing through his heartbreak, determined to find that right someone to nurse his Elizabeth until she drew her last breath.

James was faced with few prospects, and so, with little choice in the matter, he hired Minnie Pearce, a 14 year old orphan. Minnie nursed Elizabeth with tender care, but it was to no avail. Within a few months, James Kennedy's dear wife passed away. Also within a few months, the 50-year-old widower decided to take the young Minnie as his new bride. That precipitated their quick and timely move to Detroit, where they became husband and wife, and then delighted parents of a new baby girl.

Aimee Kennedy was a beautiful, talented little girl. Her mother, who had been raised by a couple in the Salvation Army, dedicated her to God's service. Aimee grew up with great ability as a public speaker and became much in demand. An independent thinker, Aimee was intrigued with Darwin's theory of evolution, and oddly enough, she had become such a skilled debater that local clergyman would not even think to tangle with the tenacious 15-year-old. Because it had been revealed that the Bible and evolution squared off against each other, Aimee decided to employ the works of Voltaire, Paine and Ingersoll as well, reveling in the knowledge that the public enjoyed her debates with learned men.

Perhaps because of her mind that sought truth, or perhaps because of the persuasive blue eyes of a new young evangelist in town, Aimee came face to face with the reality of Jesus Christ.

Up until her encounter with the handsome, 6-foot tall, brown-haired, Irish preacher, Aimee considered herself to be a died in the wool atheist. Imagine the heartbreak her poor mother must have felt, wondering what had happened to the precious baby that she had dedicated to the service of God.

There had been much talk around town that this chestnut-haired evangelist was "filled with the Holy Spirit," and Aimee decided it would be a lot of fun to spend an evening making fun of him and the simple-minded town folk.

What Aimee hadn't counted on was the truth about Jesus Christ and the awesome power of the Holy Spirit That night, Aimee experienced the outpouring of God's unfailing love and the divine Power of the Holy Spirit to change and embolden a life given unwaveringly to God. Because Aimee gave herself completely to everything in life, she abandoned her very being to the Lord and prayerfully asked what God would have of her life. The answer came back strong and clear, "Become a winner of souls." *But how could that possibly be?* she wondered. Women were not allowed to become evangelists. *How, Lord, am I to do this impossible feat?* she asked. Becoming a woman evangelist was not very likely, she thought, and besides, who in the world would encourage her to accomplish such a task?

God's providence provided the answer when Aimee ended up falling head over heels in love with the young evangelist. Robert Semple and Aimee were married on August 12, 1908, and it was just seemed the natural order of things for Aimee to assume the role of minister's wife—a wife who had been called to evangelize the world.

Through a series of events (divine appointments, if you will), Aimee was on her way to reaching the lost for Christ. Robert and Aimee raised funds to travel to China to begin their missionary work, and before their departure they made two trips, one to visit Robert's parents in Ireland and the other to visit a benefactor in London.

While in Ireland, Aimee discovered she was going to have a baby, and then while in London, she was asked by their potential benefactor, Mr. Polhill to speak before a crowd of 1,500 at a very formal evening affair at a plush theatre. At 19, Aimee was overwhelmed with the idea of speaking before such a large crowd. What in the world would she say? She had no outline of a sermon to go by and nothing was planned, but nevertheless she was willing. When her Bible opened up, a passage leapt out at her in boldface type and she felt as if an electric current had jolted through her very being. The power of the Holy Spirit fell upon her and the words flowed through her as soon as she opened her mouth to speak. The crowd was stirred with her zeal and passion, and just as suddenly as she began to preach, she stopped, much to her surprise. The revealed Power of the Holy Spirit set Aimee on the next chapter of her young life. She was electrified.

In June of 1910, Robert and Aimee arrived in China and were dismayed to find that the living conditions of the land were very unsanitary. There was much opportunity to spread the Gospel, and Robert threw himself into his work with much enthusiasm, using an interpreter to preach the Gospel to the native villagers. After a mere two months both Robert and Aimee came down with malaria and dysentery. Sadly, Robert succumbed to the illness. On August 17, 1910, he passed away quietly in his hospital bed, never to gaze upon his baby daughter that was born a month earlier to the day of his death. Aimee named the tiny but healthy baby Roberta, for her father, and then added a second name, Star, to represent the star of hope that this precious baby held for a new life.

Upon returning to the United States, Aimee moved in with her mother, who had separated from her father, unable to bear another day in the bleak, rural surroundings that she had tolerated in Canada. In New York Aimee met a 23-year-old accountant that was a no- nonsense kind of guy who fell deeply in love with her and proposed marriage. Finally consenting, she married Harold Stuart (Mack) McPherson in the spring of 1912, and on March of 1913, their son Rolf was born.

Poor Aimee soon found herself battling a different type of illness when she began experiencing deep, profound bouts of post- partum depression, huddling in corners, crying hysterically, and fervently praying for much needed relief. It was in the months after Rolf's birth that she began to hear God speaking urgently to her "Will you go?" and "Preach the Word!" It was not exactly what she wanted to hear. Nevertheless, after church meetings, talks on China, and leading Bible classes did nothing to put the call to preach to rest, she finally relented.

With all the frantic work in the effort to avoid God's call on her life, Aimee fell deathly ill, and even then the voice of the Lord sought her out with urgency. "Go! Do the works of an evangelist." Even after several surgeries, Aimee still heard the voice of God steadily calling her to preach, even after the nurses tending to her gave her up for dead, the voice came one last time, "Now will you go?"

After many months of being on the brink of death, Aimee relented, "Yes, Lord, I will go." Within two weeks she was up, vibrant and completely healed.

Aimee did not hesitate this time in answering the call and went with her mother to a Pentecostal camp meeting in Ontario. In the sweltering heat that evening Aimee received the power of the Holy Spirit after coming forward and asking for forgiveness. She began to speak powerfully in tongues, and in reaching out to others around her, they too received the Holy Spirit. The year was 1915 and it was an amazing year indeed.

Aimee's life was never the same after that camp meeting and in the years to follow she drew great crowds wherever she preached. Even standing on a street corner garnered more than fifty people who were willing to follow her at her request to hear her preach. It was nothing to have two hundred, five hundred or more in attendance when she preached the Gospel.

Aimee preached from street corners to tents, and from tents to a 1912 Packard touring car that she used to evangelize the masses. She stood in the car, using the back seat as a pulpit, and people stood on the running boards just to get close to her and touch her, weeping and confessing their sins. The traveling revivals were to continue for many years. As a result thousands were saved, healed, and changed through the love of Jesus Christ. The power of the Holy Spirit was ever present and even the hard-line press loved Aimee Semple McPherson.

But when one is used of God, sometimes controversy raises its ugly head. Change was in the air and a fresh challenge presented itself to Aimee in the way of finding a permanent place where she could preach from and prepare others for service to Christ.

With her family moved to Los Angeles, Aimee set up her new meeting place named Angelus Temple, built entirely with cash donations. The Temple, which held up to 5,000 people, cost $1.2 million and was totally debt free upon completion. Some in the "religious community" in the surrounding area and in the nation were not too happy.

Aimee posed a threat to their very livelihood, and they began to seek ways to discredit this upstart of a clergywoman. How dare she set up a church and infringe on the churches that had worked so hard to build up their congregations. But Aimee didn't let their criticisms daunt her resolution to preach Christ to those who longed to know the truth about God and the promise of eternal life.

Despite her critics, many great churches supported Aimee and a number of them even openly invited her to share the message with their people. God was using Aimee in a grand way, and so many met Christ because of her obedience to share the truth of the Gospel.

Aimee Semple McPherson was an unusual, perhaps eccentric woman, but a woman devoted to God nonetheless. History has tried to make Aimee seem almost a scam artist, a con woman or worse. These labels are false, and countless court records and reports tell the real truth concerning this amazing woman. The most controversial story is one surrounding her alleged kidnapping on the morning of May 18, 1926.

Aimee disappeared on that May morning as she and her secretary visited Ocean Park where Aimee intended to rest and write a few sermons. The account of her kidnapping was great fodder for the press, and they just could not get enough of this religious, controversial female evangelist. Aimee's rendition of the event states that as she was wading in the surf a couple approached and pleaded for her to pray for their sick child. Aimee agreed, but when she arrived at their vehicle, they pressed a chloroform-soaked cloth over her face. When she came to, she realized that she was in a small house in an unknown location far from her loved ones.

Aimee's family began to believe that she had drowned, and a search party was dispatched to look for her body. Barely a month later Aimee's mother received a ransom note asking for $500,000 for the safe return of her daughter. Minnie didn't believe this note one bit. She felt her daughter must be dead and dismissed the note as a hoax.

When Aimee was left alone by her captors she managed to escape and struggled to find help, foiling her captor's attempts to try and send a second ransom note to her mother.

The perpetrators had moved Aimee to an isolated shack in the desert. Poor Aimee was distraught, dehydrated and lost, but determined to reach help at all cost.

On June 23, Aimee collapsed on the ground in front of a house in Agua Prieta, Mexico. The homeowners were able to get a cab driver to take her to the sheriff's office across the border in Douglass, Arizona, and from there she was taken to the Calmet and Arizona Hospital. The next day Aimee was reunited with her mother and daughter, and then escorted back to L.A. by detectives from the Los Angeles Police Department. This chapter in Aimee's life would be opened up to a media feeding frenzy.

The district attorney's office called together a grand jury to investigate the kidnapping to supposedly obtain an indictment against the kidnappers. But the truth be told, they were actually looking to discredit Aimee's story. They really weren't interested in investigating the details of her account of the kidnapping, but rather looking to blame Aimee and her mother in concocting this supposed grand hoax.

The other far-fetched story was that Aimee was having an affair with a radio engineer by the name of Kenneth Ormiston.

The papers so enjoyed writing about Aimee's "love nest" in Carmel, California.

The charges against Aimee and her mother that were up for consideration were "criminal conspiracy to commit acts injurious to public morals and to prevent and obstruct justice," which threatened "the peace and dignity of the people of the State of California." This charge held the potential of a prison sentence of up to 42 years for Aimee and her mother if the grand jury could prove these preposterous allegations. It was through God's favor that Judge Jacob F. Denney dismissed the case without a jury. At last the case was finally closed, but the controversy still lingers in the minds of some even to this very day.

It was in 1927 that Aimee opened and pastored the Angelus Temple's Foursquare Commissary, an operation that met the needs of the poor and disenfranchised. Nowhere else in town could a person come to find warm clothing, blankets and food—no questions asked.

During the depression Aimee was able to feed thousands who otherwise would have starved to death. In its first month of operation the soup kitchen fed 80,000 hungry people. In addition to the soup kitchen, Aimee was able to persuade a group of physicians and dentists to set up a free clinic. She was also able to convince the Army to re-open one of its facilities to provide housing for 25,000 homeless families.

Aimee preached upwards of twenty sermons every week, plus writing, producing, and designing productions that illustrated Gospel stories. Not only that, but she wrote books, edited a magazine, composed operas, and broadcast messages on KFSG radio. It is no wonder that Aimee's health began to suffer under the pressures of all this work. Her marriage to

Harold MacPherson had ended years before he realized that he could not compete with the demands of Aimee's ministry. Harold had sued her for divorce, claiming she deserted him. Because she was very lonely, Aimee married again to an actor and singer by the name of David Hutton. This marriage lasted less than three years and stirred a lot of controversy within the church because her previous husband was still alive.

Because her health was in such a precarious condition Aimee began taking tranquilizers to rest and to help her sleep soundly. Unfortunately this would prove Aimee's undoing and final demise. Speaking to a crowd of 10,000 in Oakland, California, in 1944 Aimee found herself excited and extremely wound up. Unable to sleep, she took several of her "hypnotic sedatives" hoping to get a good night's sleep, even placing several of the pills on her pillow. Very early the next morning she awoke sweating profusely and breathing heavily. In an attempt to call two doctors, she was unable to get through and on her third call for help she lost consciousness. Aimee Semple MacPherson was pronounced dead at 11:45 a.m.

Aimee died as she had lived, in controversy. Because of the pills she had taken, there was speculation that she had committed suicide. But nothing could be further from the truth concerning this dedicated woman of God.

It is God's love that propelled Aimee to reach out to His people in need. It was the sacrifice of His beloved son Jesus Christ on the cross at Calvary that motivated Aimee to keep running the race and fighting the good fight. Because of her resolve, thousands upon thousands came to know Jesus as Lord and Savior, and because of her obedience, the International Church of the Foursquare Gospel became a new denomination, a movement that continues to grow to this very day. Aimee also began the L.I.F.E. (Lighthouse of International Foursquare

Evangelism) Bible College to equip and train young men and women for ministry.

The list of lives who were touched by Aimee will go on throughout eternity, a living breathing testimony of how God used one obedient, devoted woman to change the world.

Scripture Application

> HE SAID TO THEM,
> "GO INTO ALL THE WORLD
> AND PREACH
> THE GOOD NEWS
> TO ALL CREATION."
>
> MARK 16:15

DAHLIA RUFFLED STRAWBERRY
A BRILLIANT FLOWER FOR A BRILLIANT WOMAN OF GOD,
THIS DAHLIA MAKES A STATEMENT THAT EXUDES CONFIDENCE.
STATELY AND PROMINENT IT OCCUPIES THE GARDEN WITH A
SURETY OF INTENT, KNOWING FULL WELL ITS PURPOSE.
I KNOW WHO I AM AND WHOSE I AM—THIS WAS HENRIETTA MEARS.

Henrietta Mears

1890–1963

Mentor Extraordinaire

On the cold windblown prairie of North Dakota in 1890, one of the greatest Sunday school teachers was born, the youngest of seven children. When thinking of a Sunday school teacher one envisions a kind lady instructing a small classroom with a handful of dutiful students cajoled into attending by determined parents. But this was no ordinary Sunday school teacher. This was Dr. Henrietta Mears, a passionate, energetic woman with tremendous faith.

Henrietta accepted Christ as a young girl and began teaching her first Sunday school class at the tender age of twelve. Her love of teaching influenced her entire life, and as her profession she often taught high school chemistry or was involved in drama productions. Even though she taught students full time, she never missed her church's Sunday school program.

Henrietta's personality was as large as her passion for Christ and most of the time she could be seen wearing flamboyant hats, multiple rings, and the attention-grabbing red dresses she preferred. A bit on the chubby side, she wore thick glasses that helped to overcome her lifelong shortsightedness. Henrietta's concerned mother had been warned by doctors that her bright, eager daughter would be blind by the time she was thirty years old. But the young girl would not hear of such talk and knew that God had a purpose for her life, so she began to read, study and memorize as much of the Bible as she could, just in case her eyesight failed. Against the advice of her physicians, she enrolled in classes at the University of Minnesota, where she graduated with honors and her eyesight.

While enjoying the warm California climate on a leisure trip, Mears visited First Presbyterian Church of Hollywood. Henrietta greatly admired the ministry of the church's pastor, Dr. Stewart P. MacLennan, and much to her surprise he offered her a job in the church—not just any job, but as the Director of Christian Education overseeing the already thriving Sunday school program of 450 students.

It was 1928 and Henrietta decided that moving to sunny California was just what she needed, and to have the opportunity to serve this large Sunday school program was a wonderful challenge. Although there were a lot of activities and interest within the classes, she was disappointed and frustrated with the material available for the students. It was in this light that she decided to write her own lessons, built on solid Biblical principles. The lessons were bold, challenging and captured the essence of the principles of God's Holy Word. Armed with this new material she and her staff taught with enthusiasm and zeal to their ever-growing number of young people.

Dr. Mears' sole purpose concerning teaching was this: "Learning is more than the ability to repeat the ideas or writing of another. The purpose of the teacher is to 'draw out,' not 'cram in.' We create an interest in the heart and mind that will make the learner reach out and take hold upon the things that are taught."

The events of the next two years are recorded in church history and stand as one of the most dynamic testimonies of the twentieth century. Within two years of Dr. Mears' presentation of her Biblical principles, attendance exploded to over 4,000 students. Because of the tremendous response and success of her Sunday school classes it wasn't long before churches across the country were requesting copies of her material. It was then that Henrietta and several businessmen who attended her classes developed Gospel Light Publications in 1933, one of the first publishers of Sunday school materials in the Christian education market. Being located in the Hollywood area drew many well-known movie stars and celebrities to her studies as well.

Some of our country's finest pastors, evangelists and theologians were influenced by Henrietta Mears: men like Bill Bright, founder of Campus Crusade for Christ International and his wife, Vonette; Dick Halverson, who became Chaplain of the U.S. Senate; Dr. Bob Munger; and one of the greatest evangelists of our time, Billy Graham. Graham wrote about his beloved mentor: "I doubt if any other woman outside my wife and mother has had such a marked influence on my life. She is certainly one of the greatest Christians I have ever known!"

Henrietta never married, but she had hundreds of "spiritual" children. She was quoted as saying to them, "A bird is free in the air. Place a bird in water, and he has lost his liberty. A fish is free in the water, but leave him on the sand and he perishes. He is out of his realm. So young people, the Christian is free when he does the will of God and is obedient to God's command. This is as natural a realm for God's child as the water is for the fish, or the air for the bird."

To expand her influence in the lives of college students, Henrietta bought and directed Forest Home Conference Center in the Southern California hills in 1939. Because of her heart to educate young people, over 400 men and countless women entered into full-time Christian ministry, becoming living testimonies spurred by her unwavering faith. Her resolve to live and extol Christ-centered teachings impacted so many for the kingdom of God, we will never truly know, this side of heaven, the sheer magnitude of her godly influence.

Henrietta traveled throughout the world, not content to stay behind closed walls. "When I consider my ministry I think of the world," she proclaimed in her writings. "Anything less than that would not be worthy of Christ nor of his will for my life." She was a much sought after conference speaker and taught that knowing Christ was the most positive, energizing experience one could have. She believed that the Christ life should reflect this enthusiasm: "I think of Jesus as vital, alert, enthusiastic, full of zest and zeal, [inspiring] men to do their best, to be their highest self. I see him walking through cities, his head held high, his shoulders thrown back, bursting with good will, kindness and good faith."

Dr. Mears' continued message throughout the ages is timeless and her inspiring words resound with truth today: "Only the best possible is good enough for God."

Henrietta had a world vision and prayed with a heart full of praise to the God of all possibilities. Near the end of her life she was nearly blind and could only read with great difficulty.

Concerning this challenge she said, "My failing eyesight has been my greatest spiritual blessing. It has kept me absolutely dependent on God."

Flamboyant, larger than life, compassionate, anointed with the Holy Spirit, teacher of thousands, and devoted servant of the Most High God. This was Henrietta Mears.

More quotes from Henrietta Mears:
• "Hospitality should have no other nature than love."
• "It is difficult to steer a parked car, so get moving."

If you haven't given your all to Jesus, won't you consider living life to the fullest? Giving your all to the Maker of the universe and Master Designer of all our lives is the highest compliment we can give to our God. As Henrietta said so succinctly, "Only the best possible is good enough for God." That is why it is so important that we persevere.

Scripture Application

> JESUS SAID, "THE THIEF COMES ONLY TO
> STEAL AND KILL AND DESTROY;
> I HAVE COME THAT YOU MAY HAVE LIFE,
> AND HAVE IT TO THE FULL."
> JOHN 10:10

CHINA ROSE
A FLOWER ADORNED WITH THE SPLENDOR OF GOD.
PEERING OUT OF THE GREEN GARDEN, THIS CHINA ROSE IS EVER
WATCHFUL, WAITING AND BLESSING THOSE THAT WOULD PASS ITS WAY.
GLADYS AYLWARD WAS A CHINA ROSE, MAINTAINING A SWEET
EXPECTATION OF REACHING THE LOST WITH THE TRUTH OF JESUS CHRIST.

Gladys Aylward

1902–1970

Missionary to China

It was near London in 1902 that Gladys Aylward was born into a working class family. As a young girl she spent much of her time working as a parlor maid and thought perhaps this would be where she would spend the rest of her life, in domestic servitude. Her life was indeed to be a life of service, but not in the ways that Gladys might have thought. God had big plans for Gladys, plans to use a little lady for very grand designs.

In one story told about the young Englishwoman, it was recounted how as a young girl she had wished to be beautiful, blonde and tall like all her friends. Surely, she thought, God must have made a mistake! Gladys was less than five feet tall, and with her black hair she felt she really stuck out in the midst of all her tall, blonde girlfriends. Oh how she envied them until many years later when she realized God's purpose for her life. It was when she looked at the short, dark-haired people of China, people exactly like her, that she realized the truth of her physical being. "Oh, God," she is said to have gasped, "You knew what you were doing!"

This story about Gladys may or may not be true. Nevertheless it is true that Gladys Aylward's small stature and appearance benefited her work as a missionary in China. Of course her total dedication to God and the love she felt for her adopted country aided her in ministering to the people she came to cherish.

Gladys' journey in becoming a missionary in China began after she attended a revival meeting where she responded to the speaker's admonishment that she dedicate herself to God. While she was studying at London's China Inland Mission Center, she struggled with passing their examinations, and as she was still a probationer, she would not be allowed go. Yet she was sure God was calling her to service in China, and she began to plan just how to make this desire of the heart happen.

Determined not to let anything stand in her way in her obedience to the Father's call, Gladys decided that she would attempt to go on her own. With this resolve she continued to work as a domestic and save as much money as she possibly could. After this decision was reached, Gladys learned of an older woman missionary named Jeannie Lawson who was in need of a younger woman to assist her in her work in China. Gladys was very enthusiastic about working with Mrs. Lawson, but was dismayed to learn that her mentor would not be able to pay the ship passage. Remaining hopeful, Gladys realized that she did have enough money for train fare and began to make plans to travel across Russia on the Trans-Siberian railroad and into China.

In good faith, Gladys set out for her long, hard journey with few possessions, but with a heart brimming with hope for the future ahead. It was in the fall of 1930 that she bade London good-bye and greeted the city of Vladivostok, where she then traveled by ship to Japan, then on to China. On the last leg of her journey, Gladys rode a mule to the community of Yangchen, south of Beijing, to finally join Mrs. Lawson. But in spite of her exhilaration upon arriving in the village, she was dismayed to discover that the local people mistrusted foreigners like Mrs. Lawson and now unfortunately, Gladys as well.

Gladys rolled up her sleeves and was determined to make the very best of the situation, willing to serve in whatever capacity God and Mrs. Lawson needed. Mrs. Lawson and Gladys opened an inn to serve the many travelers that passed through Yahgchen, which was situated on a major commercial route. Traders in coal, cotton and iron goods were carried through on mule trains and their plan was to be able to evangelize the mule traders that would stop in for food and a good night's sleep. Gladys wanted to be sure they always had customers, so when they first opened she boldly approached the mule train and grabbed the harness of the lead mule to lead it right into the courtyard. Of course mules are very smart and these particular ones knew that entering such a place meant food so all the rest of the mules followed suit. The mule drivers knew not to disagree with the mules, so of course they followed along and stayed at the inn where Mrs. Lawson and Gladys provided them with plenty of hot food and comfortable beds.

Soon weary travelers knew to stop at the inn and find the much needed rest that they and their mule teams required for the journey. It was during this time that Gladys practiced her Chinese until she became fluent and could then converse with their customers. Naturally the two women were able to share many stories about a man named Jesus, and they even had a few converts as a result of their efforts. Sadly Mrs. Lawson died as the result of a serious fall and Gladys was left alone with their Chinese cook to operate the mission.

With a heart steadied to continue to be a presence and witness for Christ in China, Gladys was more than grateful when the local Mandarin paid her an official visit. His request was quite an unusual offer, asking Gladys to intervene within the upper class women's homes to inspect whether or not they were complying with the ban on foot binding.

It had been a custom for many years that young girls of the upper class families have their feet bound in a cruel and abnormal fashion. These young girls suffered with bent and shortened feet, their families deeming this as graceful and appropriate for proper beauty. But others felt this was a cruel way to control young girls in order to assure their limited mobility and therefore protect their chastity. The Mandarin wanted Gladys to investigate the local homes where as a woman she could enter freely into the women's quarters to enforce the ban. It was also because her feet were not bound and she could travel easily unhampered. Gladys saw this as an opportunity to witness and to become more of a part of the community at large.

In another instance, the Mandarin again sought Gladys to help quell a riot in a local prison. The prison guards were afraid to intervene and when the warden urged Gladys to enter the prison yard, she hesitated for a moment. The warden challenged Gladys with her own teaching concerning the Lord. "You have been preaching that those who trust in Christ have nothing to fear." With that reminder, Gladys entered the prison.

Amazingly she was able to calm the men just by listening to their grievances. There was so little for them to do in their cramped quarters and so little good food. Gladys suggested to the warden that they be given jobs where they could earn a little money for their food. The warden agreed to this idea and acquired some looms to weave cloth and a grindstone to grind grain to help meet some of the prisoners' needs. This improved the attitudes greatly, and prison conditions improved for the men. For this loving service and example Gladys was christened "Ai-weh-deh" or "Virtuous One."

Gladys lived and dressed as her neighbors, so they accepted her readily and listened to her message. Occasionally she visited the Mandarin's home where they enjoyed conversations even if he did not accept her faith. The little children were as fond of Gladys as she was of them, so when she came across a ragged, malnourished boy begging in the street it was only natural that she took him in to nurture. When the first boy brought another like him, she welcomed him cheerfully into her family. It wasn't long before she had adopted many children into her home that she believed God had sent for her to protect.

There was a deep, abiding love for China that resided in Gladys' heart, and because of this love she decided in 1936 to become a Chinese citizen. Gladys' days were devoted and busy caring for the children, never suspecting that life for them would be changed forever. In 1938 Japan declared war on China and bombed Yangchen, destroying much of the village and killing many people. The Mandarin led many of the survivors into the mountains to a hidden retreat. It was then that he shared glorious news with Gladys: He said that because of her life witness, he had decided to adopt her faith.

As the war raged on, Gladys increasingly found herself in dangerous situations, but because she was so devoted to her adopted country she readily shared any information that might help the Chinese. When she discovered that the Japanese had been sending around a circular offering a reward for her capture or death, she knew she had to escape. With this imminent threat, Gladys took the one hundred children that she had taken in and fled to a government orphanage in Sian. For a torturous twelve days they traveled, lodging at times with caring individuals and most times staying out in the elements for fear of being discovered.

With the children rallying around Gladys she felt encouragement when only despair seemed right. Even when they reached the Yellow River with no way to cross, the children raised her spirits. Because the Japanese were always on the lookout for Chinese watercraft, the local people hid their boats for fear of seizure, so crossing seemed impossible. The children urged Gladys to pray with them and sing a few songs. Their merry singing attracted a Chinese patrol, and after the leader heard their story he offered to help find them a boat. Finally with a boat secured they crossed successfully and reached the orphanage at Sian. It was a triumphant moment for the children and Gladys, but their joy was short lived when she became seriously ill with Typhus fever.

With much care and rest Gladys recovered and began to think seriously once more about her call to evangelize the people of China. It was there in Sian that Gladys established a church, continuing her outreach of ministry to the lepers near the borders of Tibet. Her heart was still one of service to God, but when she discovered that her many injuries from the war had taken a toll on her health and had left her somewhat disabled, she realized it was now too much of a challenge. Because she could also see that the Communists were now an ever-growing presence in China, she reluctantly decided it was time to return to her native England.

It was post-war 1947, and Gladys could not settle comfortably in England for long. So, despite her impairments she settled into a new life in Taiwan where she set up an orphanage. Living out her promise to God to dedicate her life to him in service, Gladys Aylward died in 1970 in Taiwan, still serving the children he had sent her to care for and rescue from harm's way.

The world learned of this little woman in a big way when in 1957 Alan Burgess published Gladys' story as *The Small Woman*. Later it became a Hollywood movie, *The Inn of the Sixth Happiness*, starring Ingrid Bergman as a much taller Gladys.

One cannot help but admire such an amazing woman of courage and faith, a small woman who trusted her Lord to overcome much and achieve grand, big things for Him! Like Gladys we must trust God instead of our own abilities, physical strength, or wisdom. It is by becoming like little children, trusting, obeying and loving our heavenly Father that we are able to overcome obstacles and achieve great things for Jesus. It is by our daily submission to Him that we are able to live a life of significance.

Scripture Application

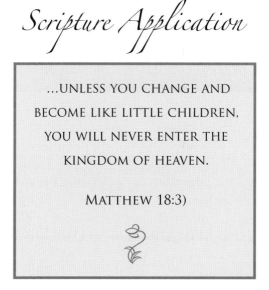

...UNLESS YOU CHANGE AND
BECOME LIKE LITTLE CHILDREN,
YOU WILL NEVER ENTER THE
KINGDOM OF HEAVEN.

MATTHEW 18:3)

AGAPANTHUS
THIS AMAZING FLOWER HAS A WAY OF JUMPING OUT AND SAYING,
"SEE ME? I KNOW MY PURPOSE AND WHAT PLEASES THE CREATOR.
I ATTRACT THOSE WHO HUNGER AND THIRST FOR THAT WHICH WOULD
GIVE LIFE AND NOURISHMENT. GOD GAVE SUCH A DESIRE AND
PURPOSE TO ELIZA SHIRLEY.

Eliza Shirley

1863 - 1945

Founder of The Salvation Army in America

In Coventry, England, in 1863 Eliza Shirley was born to Amos and Annie Shirley and raised in a proper Victorian home. Growing up in 19th century England with all the customs and manners that accompanied her station in life was not exactly what young Eliza yearned for. An ordinary, middle class life just did not seem to excite or lift her spirits, but she wasn't quite sure what she was supposed to do with her life.

Amos Shirley was a part-time preacher, and even at a young age, Eliza memorized her father's sermons and relished the teaching the scriptures provided. When she was just fifteen years old, a group of Salvation Army women marched into her hometown and became known as the Hallelujah Lassies. These wonderful women of God took to holding meetings right out in front of taverns in the poorest of neighborhoods. Their preaching so captivated Eliza that she determined that she too would become a Salvation Army worker, dedicating her life to God's service. Her heart's deepest desire was to bring the saving grace of Jesus Christ to the poorest of the poor, those whom society abandoned. Amos and Annie Shirley also participated in the Salvation Army meetings, but they convinced fifteen-year-old Eliza to wait until her sixteenth birthday before joining the Hallelujah Lassies.

Upon passing her sixteenth birthday, Eliza responded to a summons by the General of the Salvation Army, William Booth, to review her request for full-time service into the evangelical group. General Booth readily accepted her petition and assigned her to a post in Bishop Aukland, a coal-mining village in Northern England.

This petite, pretty young girl joined in service with another lovely Hallelujah Lassie, Annie Allspop, and together they endured unfathomable poverty in this tiny mining village. Most of their food was attained by keeping what the villagers threw at them during open air meetings, and any money garnered from these meetings was stolen by the crowds before it ever reached them. It truly was amazing that these two sweet girls were able to endure such extreme hardship, but through their patience and love, the village was soon won for Christ. They witnessed God moving in a mighty way in this tough community and through the power of Jesus Christ even the worst men were converted during their meetings. Eliza and Annie persevered and lives were changed.

It was sometime later that year that Eliza's father Amos entreated her to consider immigrating with them to America. Amos Shirley even suggested that she meet with General Booth to ask if he would endorse her to begin the Salvation Army in America. General Booth was at first a bit hesitant in approving

Eliza's petition, but he then gave her his blessing to go and report back on what she found in the states.

Eliza, Amos and Annie Shirley arrived in Philadelphia in 1880 to begin their ambitious work for the souls of America. After looking about for a building for their meetings, they settled in an abandoned chair factory, only to have a mere 12 people show up for their first attempt to attract a following. They tried holding open air meetings in the street a few blocks away from the factory, but the police put a stop to their meeting because of the rowdy, rough crowds that pummeled them with rotten vegetables, mud, stones and sticks.

God had great mercy on the Shirleys and after four agonizing weeks, they found a lot where they could hold open air meetings. On the first night that they were to launch their meeting they noticed a glow in the sky as they approached. Someone had started a fire in a tar barrel on the lot and a large crowd in the hundreds had turned out to watch the spectacle. Always ready to seize an opportunity, the Shirleys took the moment to preach and sing, trying to draw the crowd in and keep them there. It was after the singing and preaching that a drunk known as Reddy approached them and asked if God would forgive an old drunk like him. The love of Christ shone brightly in this little family, and because of their faithfulness, Reddy received Jesus as his Savior, and his whole life was changed.

The ministry in Philadelphia was changed as well because of Reddy's living testimony to the glory of God. The meeting house filled consistently with great throngs of people who clamored to see how the power of God could change a drunk like Reddy. They just had to see it for themselves.

Eliza was able to find another building on the west side of Philadelphia to continue the work of this fledgling ministry in America. Soon General Booth had to send more reinforcements to help the Salvation Army spread the Good News of Jesus Christ throughout America.

Sadly, Eliza's father Amos met an untimely death as the result of an accident not many years after arriving in America. In spite of their personal loss, Eliza and her mother Annie valiantly carried on with the good work they had all begun in Philadelphia. After a long rest in England, Eliza returned to America with a new husband, Captain Philip Symmonds and enjoyed a long life well into her eighties. Retiring to Chicago Eliza became an ardent Cubs fan, so much so that on her death bed as she slipped in and out of consciousness, she alternated praying with asking how the Cubs were doing in the final games of the World Series. Upon her death, Eliza Shirley Symmonds was given a moment of silence from the team and all their fans. Eliza had been promoted from the Army to eternal life with her precious Savior, Jesus Christ.

Scripture Application

> THEREFORE, MY DEAR
> BROTHERS, STAND FIRM.
> LET NOTHING MOVE YOU.
> ALWAYS GIVE YOURSELVES
> FULLY TO THE WORK
> OF THE LORD, BECAUSE
> YOU KNOW THAT YOUR
> LABOR IN THE LORD
> IS NOT IN VAIN.
>
> 1 CORINTHIANS 15: 58)

DAFFODIL

THE DAFFODIL CATCHES BOTH HEART AND MIND OFF GUARD WITH ITS
BURST OF LIFE AND JOY. THE MINUTE DETAILS WITHIN THE DAFFODIL
LEAVE ONE MARVELING AT EVERY NUANCE OF THIS FORMIDABLE PLANT.
THESE SAME DETAILS OF OUR WALK WITH JESUS CHRIST WERE CAPTURED
THROUGH FANNY CROSBY'S LIFE AND MANY HYMNS.

Fanny Crosby

1820 - 1920

Mother of Hymns

Frances Jane (Fanny) Crosby was born on March 24, 1820 into a family of devout Puritans in Southeast Putnam County, New York. John and Mercy Crosby doted on their new baby girl, but at just six weeks of age she was stricken with an inflammation in both eyes. Having been born with normal vision, Fanny's parents felt assured that their family doctor would have the inflammation resolved in no time. But upon finding that their doctor was not available they sought help from a man who was purported to be a medically qualified individual. Much to their alarm this "doctor" placed hot mustard poultices on their baby daughter's eyes that left them scarred and sightless. Not surprisingly this imposter left town in great haste, leaving the Crosby family devastated.

More tragedy would befall the little family when Fanny's father died when she was just 12 months old. Left with little resource, her 21-year-old mother sought work as a domestic in a nearby town, leaving her baby daughter with her mother, Eunice, to nurture and care for as her own.

Grandma Eunice was a staunch believer in independence and determined early on that Fanny would not be relegated to the care of others, forever dependent because of her blindness. Rather she set out to liberate her granddaughter's mind through the world around her, especially through memorizing books and extensive portions of the Bible. Before she was 10 years old Fanny had memorized most of the New Testament and more than five books of the Old Testament.

As Fanny grew, her Grandmother insisted she be treated as "normal" as possible and encouraged her to play with the other children and experience as much as she could. When told by a variety of physicians that Fanny would never regain her sight or care for herself, Eunice became more determined than ever to help her granddaughter.

Fanny was eager to try and fit in and attended nearby schools in hopes of learning with the other children. However, this arrangement never worked very well as the teachers and student faced frustration in efforts to further her education. This was very discouraging to Fanny, who was a very bright girl. But instead of languishing in her situation she prayed and asked God to use her, resisting the notion that her blindness would somehow relegate her life to nothingness.

This confidence and fresh sense of purpose was proclaimed mightily in her first poem when she was eight years old:

O what a happy soul am I!
Although I cannot see, I am resolved that in this world,
Contented I will be,

How many blessings I enjoy,
That other people don't.
To weep and sigh because I'm blind,
I cannot and I won't!

It became evident that Fanny possessed an ever-expansive mind, filled with creative and vibrant stirrings. Her voice was expressive, she played the piano well, and she garnered a lot of popularity locally for her gift of writing poetry. Opportunity for the possibility of further schooling for her appeared when her mother heard about the opening of The New York Institute for the Blind. This new school was exactly what Fanny had been praying for. In 1835, she enrolled and there she found her chance to achieve her dreams through the people who could teach her all that her heart longed to learn.

Fanny immersed herself in school work by listening to lectures, readings and hearing teachings on a variety of subjects taught at regular schools. Lessons on English, grammar, science, music, history, philosophy and astronomy filled her mind with endless possibilities for the future. Fanny learned very quickly and so completely that she could recite entire contents of her grammar text many years later.

Fanny became a teacher at the institute in 1847, continuing to demonstrate her poetic ability when asked to compose verses for special occasions and to honor prominent guests. Through this role as the institution's poetess, Fanny became acquainted with many celebrated notables, such as President James K. Polk, Presidents Tyler and Van Buren, Jenny Lind, the famed singer, Henry Clay, General Winfield Scott and even newspaper man Horace Greeley. She was quite honored when he asked her to provide poems for his widely circulated newspaper. Another longtime admirer who copied her poems and became her lifelong friend was none other than Grover Cleveland.

Fanny's love for poetry continued and in 1844 she published a collection of her verse as *The Blind Girl and Other Poems*, a second volume was issued in 1849 entitled *Monterey, and Other Poems*, followed in 1849 with *A Wreath of Columbia's Flowers*, with many more volumes to follow.

Even though Fanny's Grandmother Eunice taught her eager granddaughter Christian values and disciplines, it wasn't until November 20, 1850, that she became a Christian. After witnessing more than half the students at the institute succumb to a severe cholera epidemic in 1849, she was deeply troubled and shaken. Ministering to the overwhelming needs of the sick and dying, she realized that she had narrowly escaped death herself and it was this encounter with mortality that led her to surrender to her Lord and Savior Jesus Christ. It was at a revival at the old John Street Methodist Church in New York that her conversion occurred. As the grand old consecration hymn "Alas! And Did My Savior Bleed" reached the third line of the fifth stanza—"Here, Lord, I give myself away"—"My very soul was flooded with celestial light." Fanny said. The God of her grandmother had become real to her.

While still working at the Institute she began to openly enjoy the company of fellow instructor Alexander Van Alystyne, a somewhat younger but talented and accomplished musician. They had actually fallen in love when they were both still students at the school, marrying in 1858 when she was 38 and he 27. The young couple then made the difficult decision to leave the Institute soon after their marriage, mostly due to the deteriorating conditions and relationships within the school.

It would seem that Fanny would now have the life that she had prayed for, a husband, home, and soon to be family. Their only child was born in 1858, but died soon after birth. The baby was rarely, if ever, mentioned again, and the details of the baby's birth were so vague that it was unclear whether the progeny was a boy or a girl. Whether for this reason or some other, she and "Van" as she called her husband, followed separate career paths and eventually lived apart, staying married, but remaining very good friends until his death in 1902.

Fanny's deep and abiding faith brought her much comfort and peace as she grieved the loss of her baby. God was the mainstay of her existence and Fanny found herself a part of the burgeoning religious revival that was sweeping the nation. With her spirit soaring, Fanny burst forth onto the church scene by providing lyrics for the newly developed Sunday school programs for adults. These schools evolved from the effort to offer secular education to working men on Sundays that eventually evolved into the church's education ministry.

The preference for more loving, personal Sunday school or later Gospel songs over the traditional and much more solemn hymns resulted in lyricists like Fanny and composers such as William Bradbury gaining much popularity with their compositions.

It was an inspired and divine appointment of God when Fanny's pastor, Peter Stryker, introduced her to William Bradbury, an internationally acclaimed composer who had performed widely in Europe as well as America. William had great difficulty in finding the right material for his compositions and was always looking for suitable lyrics for his work. When Fanny submitted her first Christian hymn to him in three days, with the beginning stanza "We are going, we are going beyond the skies, where the fields are robed in beauty, and the sunlight never dies," Bradbury knew that he had found his new lyricist. Fanny was now 44 years old and together they formed a business and personal association within his publishing company. She also enjoyed great success by collaborating with businessman and part-time composer William Doan, who would become a close friend for more than forty years.

William Doan would often ask Fanny to come up with the lyrics to an idea, melody or title he had come up with, and most of the time she was right on the money. Once though, he asked that she come up with lyrics to go with the phrase "Pass Me Not, O Gentle Savior," but she struggled for inspiration. Only when she was speaking at a prison, a short time later, and heard an inmate shout, "Good Lord, don't pass me by!" were the words kindled in her spirit. After Doan provided the melody, this hymn was used at this same prison, inspiring several conversions to Christ.

Another time Doan was on his way to catch a train and stopped at Fanny's home with a most urgent request. He had a melody on his mind and was in need of a poem to fit the tune. As she listened to the tune, she clapped her hands together and exclaimed in excitement. "That says 'Safe in the Arms of Jesus'!" And after a time of private prayer she returned to dictate the entire poem, much to the delight of William Doan. This beautiful hymn touched those who had lost a child—as Fanny had—and became an instant success, even gaining worldwide popularity.

Once more Fanny met Doan's need of inspirational words to fit a particularly moving melody when she accepted his invitation to address an audience. While speaking she paused to describe an impression she had. "There's a dear boy here who has wandered away from his mother's teaching. Would he please come to me at the close of the service?" A young man did come forward at the end of the service and shared with Fanny how he had promised his mother that he would meet her in heaven, but because of the way he had been living, he wasn't sure that he would. Then after a time of prayer, the newly converted boy became jubilant. "I've found my mother's God and I'll meet her in heaven!" The song "Rescue the Perishing" then took form to William Doan's moving melody. With the young man's exuberant realization that his promise to his mother was now kept, inspiration had taken root in Fanny's heart and spirit and the words flooded her being.

Another divine appointment of God came in 1876 when Fanny met Dwight L. Moody, the well-renowned evangelist of her time and his featured soloist, Ira Sankey. From this meeting came a long professional and personal relationship with both men that lasted a lifetime. Recognizing that Fanny's gifts could become a vital part of their ministry, Sankey published many of her hymns as well as providing music for her verses. It was a match made in heaven.

Although Fanny would never receive much money, sometimes only a few dollars, for all her inspired, hard work, she never once complained. Fanny described her hymns as a "song of the heart addressed to God" feeling that her work was for God and her reward was the effect it had on the listeners that came to Him. She did not agree with those that felt she was being exploited by publishers that only gave her a mere pittance for her many works. It was her joy to provide the verses that lifted a melody into the hearts of those who hungered to know God, and to know him in a deeper way.

At her publisher's insistence, Fanny sometimes used pseudonyms, including initials or labels such as "the Children's Friend" or even such symbols as asterisks and number signs. One reason for this strange request from her publishers was that they didn't want it known that they relied on one person for such a volume of work. Under contract with Bigelow and Main for many years, Fanny's prolific writing produced 5,900 poems for them and in her declining years of health they provided a regular allowance for her care.

Ever the constant minister of the Gospel through her lyrics and poems, Fanny continued traveling on speaking tours and home mission work as she grew older. But as she entered her nineties she became content to stay closer to home, residing with a niece in Bridgeport, Connecticut. Fanny was lovingly called the "Queen of the Gospel Song" and often regaled her constant stream of visitors, who wanted an autograph, with a song or two. Holding court in the parlor, with her humor still intact, she sat at the piano and began with a classical tune, then crossed over to ragtime, surprising her guests when she "pepped things up" with a jazzed up version of one of her hymns!

Even towards the very end of her life Fanny was still concerned for the well-being of others, and when a neighbor family grieved the loss of their child, she dictated a letter of sympathy that assured them that their daughter was "Safe in the Arms of Jesus." Later that night as she slept, the angels came and escorted her into the presence of her Savior, the Lord of her life that she had served with all her heart, all her soul and all her mind. It was February 11, 1915, and Fanny had slipped quietly away to splendor.

As the canopy of stars crept out that night, one can only imagine the singing that was occurring in the heavens the very moment that Fanny stepped into the presence of our Most Holy God. Such a stir in the Kingdom was surely to have taken place as she looked about at the glorious assembly on high. Yes, of course, for now dear Frances Jane Crosby could finally see the magnificence that she had so inspirationally created verse and lyrics for—wonderful words of life. Her words, like Fanny, will live with her Savior throughout eternity.

Scripture Application

> BUT AS FOR ME; I WILL ALWAYS
> HAVE HOPE; I WILL PRAISE YOU
> MORE AND MORE.
>
> PSALM 71:14
>
> THE PATH OF THE RIGHTEOUS
> IS LIKE THE FIRST GLEAM OF
> DAWN, SHINING EVER BRIGHTER
> TILL THE FULL LIGHT OF DAY.
>
> PROVERBS 4:18

CLEMATIS RED CARDINAL
THIS ATTRACTIVE FLOWER OF STRIKING BEAUTY MAKES A BOLD
STATEMENT IN ITS PRESENTATION AND LINGERING IMPACT. NOT EASILY
MISSED IN THE GARDEN, IT SPEAKS OF THE SHED BLOOD OF CHRIST
ON CALVARY, JOYFULLY PROCLAIMING THAT WE LIVE BECAUSE HE DIED.
SUSANNAH SPURGEON LIVED THIS VERY WAY THROUGHOUT
HER ENTIRE LIFE.

Susannah Spurgeon

1832-1892

Wife of Charles Spurgeon
Mother and Spiritual Nurturer

Susannah Spurgeon was born Susannah Thompson on January 15, 1832 to godly parents in the southern suburbs of London. Mr. and Mrs. R. B. Thompson raised their daughter with sound Christian principles, and at a young age Susannah accepted Christ. Oddly enough, Susannah and her friends, though believers in Christ, did not actively pursue Christian service or further their knowledge of the Bible or their relationship with God. In her day there was no formal Sunday school or youth program that would have encouraged Susannah and her friends in developing their faith.

Susannah began to grow very indifferent and cold toward the things of faith, so when her friends talked her into joining them at the famous New Park Street Chapel in London, she balked. It wasn't exactly what she would have preferred to do, but on their insistence she reluctantly joined them to listen to a young preacher share the Gospel message. Because she had grown so spiritually cold, she didn't understand the clarity of the preaching she heard that day. The young preacher was only 19 years old, and she was not impressed with his preaching or his message.

Through her close friends Mr. and Mrs. Olney, who were members of the New Park Street Chapel, Susannah had the opportunity to see this young pastor often as he had just accepted the pastorate at the Olney's church. It was during these leisurely visits at her friend's home that she got to know Charles Spurgeon and came to regard him in an entirely new and more favorable light. Through their conversations Susannah became aware that her Christian life was not what it should be and she soon realized just how far her walk in the faith had fallen. When Pastor Charles heard that Susannah had expressed a desire to strengthen her Christian faith he gave her an illustrated copy of *The Pilgrim's Progress* to help her along that path. Just knowing that he was genuinely concerned for her impressed her a great deal, and from that moment on their friendship grew until it had blossomed into an endearing love for one another. Susannah and Charles were married on January 5, 1856.

On September 20, 1856, their love was celebrated with the birth of healthy twin boys to complete their little family. Susannah was joyful at the birth of her babies, but the birth process had taken a toll on her physically. She was never again the picture of health she once had been. Sadly she suffered physically for much of her adult life with various ailments, bedridden for long periods of time.

In spite of her illness, Susannah was a devoted mother and brought up her two sons in the Christian faith, teaching them sound Biblical doctrine. To her immense joy she was able to see both accept Christ at an early age. As grown men they publicly acknowledged their mother's Christian instruction and how much her loving example played a part in their early conversion. They knew their mother's godly influence charted the course of their eternal destiny.

When Susannah was presented with a copy of her husband's first volume of *Lectures to My Students*, he asked her opinion. She immediately told her husband that she would place a volume in the hands of every minister in England. To that he replied, "Then why not do so: how much will you give?"

Not being prepared for this question, Susannah knew she was faced with a challenge to see if she could spare any of her housekeeping money or personal account to fulfill his wish. As she pondered this challenge, she remembered that she had put away some extra money that was left over from her monthly expenses. Retiring to her room she retrieved the money and upon tallying it up she realized she had enough money to purchase one hundred copies of the work. In that very instant the Book Fund was born.

Charles Spurgeon published a magazine called the *The Sword and the Trowel*, and in the very next issue there contained an announcement of Mrs. Spurgeon's intention of giving out the books and inviting poor Baptist ministers to apply for the book. Susannah was overwhelmed when the numerous requests for the free volume numbered much more than the anticipated one hundred she planned to distribute. That very first gifting turned out to be two hundred instead of the one she had originally proposed, and husband and wife knew they had to place another announcement in the magazine. In the following issue Charles informed his readers of the many pastors that requested the book in order to increase their knowledge and improve their ministries. He also told of Susannah's idea to create the Book Fund in order to raise the necessary funds to provide books to these needy ministers.

Susannah actually became a writer and possessed a rare literary gift, writing several books in her lifetime, including *Ten Years of My Life in the Service of the Book Fund*, *Ten Years After*, and several devotional books. Her most treasured work was C. H. Spurgeon's autobiography, which she compiled from his letters, records and diary.

Susannah enjoyed a full life raising her boys, supporting her husband in his ministry, writing and most of all overseeing the Book Fund. For the rest of her life Susannah continued the work of the Book Fund. Her last lingering thoughts before her death were for the Book Fund and for the poor ministers who so needed the books that would help instruct them in reaching others for Christ. It was her desire to leave a sum of money for the continued efforts of the Book Fund, and in her will that is exactly what Mrs. Spurgeon determined. She died as she lived, thinking only of her service to others, a heart warmed by the glow of the Master's love.

Scripture Application

I SAID TO THE LORD,
"YOU ARE MY LORD;
APART FROM YOU
I HAVE NO GOOD THING."
AS FOR THE SAINTS
WHO ARE IN THE LAND,
THEY ARE THE GLORIOUS
ONES IN WHOM IS
ALL MY DELIGHT.

PSALM 16:2-3

NEW YORK ROSE
THIS STATE FLOWER RADIATES WITH THE GLORY OF GOD,
OFFERING UP NOT ONE BUT SEVERAL BUDS OF PROMISE AND HOPE.
THOUGH THE ROSE SEEMS DELICATE, BE CAREFUL OF THE THORNS THAT
SHIELD AND PROTECT. ANNE HUTCHINSON WAS DESIGNED BY THE
CREATOR IN JUST THE SAME FORM, RESILIENT, STRONG AND DISTINCT.

Anne Hutchinson

1591–1642

Puritan Woman of Spiritual Truths

In 1591 Anne Marbury was born in Alford, Lincolnshire, England to an outspoken clergyman, the Reverend Francis Marbury, and her mother, Bridget Dryden. Her father served in the Church of England where his chief concern with the Church was that it consistently appointed unqualified ministers to serve many congregations. Because of his increasing complaints he was jailed twice until he ceased to be so vocal about the situation. Anne was inspired by her father's impassioned doctrine and she immersed herself in his many volumes of theological works and set about to live her life soundly dedicated to his example of faith and courage.

Anne's strength, passion and independence would serve her well in her adult life. When she was 21 she married Will Hutchinson and began a family. The Puritan movement was underway and a minister by the name of John Cotton was at the helm, supporting the movement. Anne was very drawn to this minister of conviction and began to listen to the ideals of the Puritan movement

King Henry VIII had established the Church of England, splitting from the powerful Catholic church in Rome, a rather risky matter, some would speculate. The King felt he had no choice in the matter as he desired to divorce his current wife and remarry the woman he hoped would provide the son and heir that would eventually rule England. In spite of the split from Catholicism, England had lived through a Protestant boy-King, an adamantly Catholic queen, and a more moderate protestant queen who diligently worked to reduce the animosity between her Catholic and Protestant subjects. Many in England believed that the Church of England still had too many Catholic doctrines and too much Catholic influence and wanted to purify their religious worship. Thus Puritans became the name they were known by. The Puritans' movement only brought more contention into the conflict surrounding the proper way to worship God.

John Cotton advocated Puritan doctrines and planted hope in the hearts and minds of those who came to hear him speak, about the possibility of immigrating to the new world, America, to practice religious freedom. Anne Hutchinson, her husband and children traveled several miles from their home to hear John Cotton preach and heard his impassioned pledge to liberate the people from the Church of England. Not only would this new world provide religious freedom for the people, he assured them that there would be economic gain as well. This message intrigued Anne and her husband Will, so when Cotton led a group to the new Puritan-based colony at Massachusetts Bay in 1634, the Hutchinson family pledged to join. They would not be alone on the treacherous journey, for more than 21,000 other Puritans immigrated to America from 1630 to 1642 to begin life anew in this untamed world.

The Puritans also advocated a simpler system of worship with fewer sacraments and worked to "purify" the church from what they felt was too much of a Catholic influence. They also wanted to be known for their example of faith to the world and that meant there had to be strictly enforced rules of conduct. Once in Massachusetts, they set a Puritan church-centered government in place and began to take seriously their resolve to be a "city on a hill." They would not tolerate any deviation from their church rules and beliefs, subsequently becoming a colony of imposed piety and oppression.

Anne did not start out to publicly voice her views on Puritan beliefs that did not set right with her understanding of the Gospel message. She lived for years quietly observing her faith, only sharing her thoughts within her family confines. It became a regular occasion for other women to gather in Anne's home to discuss the week's sermon and other biblical topics. Because Anne was brilliant, articulate and learned in the Bible and theology, women enjoyed the lively, intellectual stimulation from their conversations, and eventually many more joined their circle. The meetings grew in number, and literally hundreds of women (aided by her reputation as a skilled midwife) and even some men attended. The colonial government became alarmed. It wasn't that they minded that the women met to pray and to edify one another through godly study. It was the course and manner of assembly that disturbed the leaders enough to take serious action. It was most distasteful to them that one woman could have so much influence on a group of so many women and, most disturbingly, men as well, leading in a demonstrative, prophetic manner. It was not a woman's place to participate in this inappropriate behavior; rather she was only to be concerned with her duties as a wife and mother. It was also a well-known fact that women neither had the intellect nor the capacity to teach, not having the perception necessary to deal with theology.

Among the men of note that joined in the weekly meetings was none other than Sir Henry Vane, who became governor of the colony in 1636. When Anne, with the aid of Governor Vane and John Cotton, attempted to have her brother-in-law John Wheelwright installed as minister of the Boston church, most of the congregation supported her. But the pastor of the church, Reverend John Wilson, gave a speech on the "inevitable dangers of separation" caused by religious dissensions, and he joined with John Winthrop in opposing her.

Anne's ideas were branded as the heresy of "Antinomianism" (a belief that Christians are not bound by moral law), and her followers became know as "Antinomians." Intended to be derogatory, the term was erroneously applied to Anne's followers, who did not believe that the inner Holy Spirit released them from obligation to moral law. Still the colonial government moved to discipline her and her numerous followers in Boston. In May 1637, Vane lost the governorship to John Winthrop. To prevent new Antinomians from settling, he imposed a restriction on immigrants, among them Anne's brother and several of her friends. In August, eighty-two "heresies" committed by the Antinomians were read at a synod, and a ban was placed on all private meetings.

Anne was first charged with conducting disorderly meetings and was ordered to stop these gatherings at once. It wasn't just that she spoke against their basic understanding of doctrine; she claimed to personally have the Holy Ghost dwelling within her as a justified person of faith. Her differences sparked outrage as she continued to speak on her understanding of grace and the fact that nothing of sanctification can help to evidence to believers their justification. Her message was Christ Jesus and nothing more, a radical idea to the Puritans of her day, and they would not, could not, stand by and allow this heretical woman to make these claims. The fact that she was a widely respected and loved woman who put her Christian faith into action helping neighbors did nothing to dissuade the officials from accusing her of sedition.

John Wheelwright continued to preach and Anne now held her meetings twice a week. In November, Winthrop and his supporters filed charges against Anne and Wheelwright, who were then put on trial for heresy before a meeting of the General Court. Intending to prove that Anne's behavior was immoral, Winthrop described her meetings as "a thing not tolerable nor comely in the sight of God, nor fitting for your sex," and accused her of breaking the Fifth Commandment by not honoring her father and mother (in this case the magistrates of the colony).

At this trial, she parried all questions so well that Edmund S. Morgan, a biographer of Gov. John Winthrop, was led to comment that Anne Hutchinson was the governor's "intellectual superior in everything except political judgment; in everything except the sense of what was possible in the world." Anne came close to clearing herself of all charges, deftly answering each question. When she suddenly mentioned that she had experienced several revelations and that the Lord revealed himself to her, she said, "Upon a Throne of Justice, and all the world appearing before Him, though I must come to New England, yet I must not fear nor be dismayed," she said. "Therefore, take heed. For I know that for this that you go about to do unto me," she threatened, "God will ruin you and your posterity and this whole State." Winthop immediately replied, "I am persuaded that the revelation she brings forth is delusion." The Puritans taught that there was no divine revelation from God after the Bible was closed, and so she was sentenced to banishment from the colony, deemed "being a woman not fit for our society." All of this just for expressing her religious freedom, a right all Americans have come to treasure, and a right established eventually in our Constitution by our founding fathers.

At first Anne had a contingency of support among the colonists, but gradually this too faded and even John Cotton came to criticize her when she came to trial. Wheelwright was exiled and shortly left for New Hampshire while Anne was put under house arrest for the winter. On March 15, 1638, Anne was brought to trial before the elders of the church of Boston. When her sons and son-in-law tried to speak on her behalf, John Cotton cautioned them against "hindering" the work of God in healing her soul. To the women of the congregation he said to be careful in listening to her, "for you see she is but a woman and many unsound and dangerous principles are held by her."

Cotton, who was once her friend, now turned spitefully against her, attacking her meetings as a "promiscuous and filthy coming together of men and women without distinction of relations of marriage," and accused her of believing in free love. "Your opinions fret like a gangrene and spread like a leprosy, and will eat out the very bowels of religion."

When her excommunication was handed down, it came from Reverend Wilson, whom she had tried to have removed from Boston Church. "I do cast you out and in the name of Christ I do deliver you up to Satan that you may learn no more to blaspheme, seduce, and to lie."

"The Lord judgeth not as man judgeth," she retorted, "Better to be cast out of church than to deny Christ."

After her sentence of banishment was handed down, Anne Hutchinson, her husband, children and 60 followers settled in the land of Narragansett, where they purchased the island of Aquidneck (Peaceable Island), now Rhode Island, from Chief Miantonomah. The settlers founded a town in March of 1638, christening it Pocasset, the Indian name for that locality; the name "Portsmouth" was given to the settlement in 1639. Here they established that colony's first civil government, constructing their first meeting house. The colony was led by William Coddington and, to a degree, spiritually led by Anne Hutchinson. They, along with Samuel Gorton, each had their own followers.

The Portsmouth colony was based more on farming than on religion, with large farms growing corn, peas, beans and tobacco. Livestock was being raised, and it soon became evident that it would be necessary to develop a port to ship produce out. In addition, there developed religious differences between some of the leaders of the colony.

William Coddington had been a very wealthy man in Boston and among the political leaders there. He had been a member of the Boston Court that had expelled Roger Williams. Coddington was in William's view "a worldly man" who was most concerned about his own profit and power. He later was to adopt the religious beliefs of the Quakers.

Eventually, because of the need for a deep water port and because of the religious differences in Portsmouth, Coddington, Clarke, Nicholas Easton, and William Baulston moved south and established Newport. Five other leaders followed suit. By the end of that first year, 93 people were residents of Newport, and its numbers were growing dramatically.

Meanwhile in Portsmouth, William Hutchinson was elected leader of the settlement. He seemed a mild-mannered man, no doubt easily persuaded by Anne's strength and fortitude. It is said that even though Portsmouth had been founded on the desire for religious freedom, not one church had been erected there. Anne continued to hold weekly religious services in her home while living in Portsmouth, and her husband Will was elected assistant to Governor Coddington of the Rhode Island Colony in 1640 and died in 1642.

After her husband's death, Anne took her children, except for five of the eldest, to the Dutch colony in New York, fearing that the Massachusetts Bay authorities would try to gain control of the Portsmouth settlement. But a few months later, because the Dutch had antagonized the nearby village that year, the Indians rose up and attacked settlements beyond the walled protection of New Amsterdam (New York City) and fifteen Dutchmen were killed. In August 1643, the Siwanoy Indians led by Chief Wampage raided the Hutchinson house and slaughtered Anne and five of her youngest children. Susanna, one of her young daughters, was taken captive, living with her abductors for about four years, surviving the brutal massacre, an event that some said was divine retribution and judgment.

There is a widely held view by some historians that the Puritan fathers felt they had no discourse other than banishing Anne Hutchinson and her family. Their main concern was keeping unity within the colony, understanding that any division would harm their chances of survival in the new world. Living in a remote wilderness brought many extreme situations to the colonists and one of their biggest fears was to have someone challenge their authority, thereby limiting their control of the people and their safety.

The Puritan officials excommunicated Anne because of all these charges. However, some hold the view that Anne Hutchinson was a woman of courage who demonstrated her beliefs in a way that Christ would have supported. She lovingly taught the truth of the Gospel in order to free those who sought to know the truth, in spite of the consequences.

In what is now Pelham Bay Park (the Bronx today) within the limits of New York City, less than a dozen miles from the City Hall, is the site of Anne's house and scene of her murder. Not far from it, beside the road, is a large glacial boulder, popularly called Split Rock. The rock is so named for its division into two parts, probably the action of frost aided by the growth of a large tree, the stump of which separates the parts. The line of vision of one looking through the split towards Hutchinson River at the foot of the hill will very nearly cross the site of the house. In 1911 a bronze tablet in memory of Mrs. Hutchinson was placed on Split Rock by the Society of Colonial Dames of the State of New York, who recognized that the resting place of this most noted woman of her time was well worthy of such a memorial. The tablet bears the following inscription:

ANNE HUTCHINSON

BANISHED FROM THE MASSACHUSETTS BAY COLONY IN 1638
BECAUSE OF HER DEVOTION TO RELIGIOUS LIBERTY
THIS COURAGEOUS WOMAN SOUGHT
FREEDOM FROM PERSECUTION IN NEW NETHERLAND
NEAR THIS ROCK IN 1643 SHE AND HER HOUSEHOLD
WERE MASSACRED BY INDIANS
THIS TABLE IS PLACED HERE BY
THE COLONIAL DAMES OF THE STATE OF NEW YORK
ANNO DOMINI MCMXI
VIRTUTES MAJORUM FILLAE CONSEVANT

Some observers credit Anne Hutchinson with being the first American woman to lead the public fight for religious diversity and female equality. It is reported that Eleanor Roosevelt began her list of America's greatest women with Anne Hutchinson. Anne did indeed use her considerable influence as a woman to test the Massachusetts Bay Colony's religious tolerance, which, ironically, had been the reason for the settlement in the first place.

Dear God, may we live our lives as Anne Hutchinson did, adhering to scriptural truths in spite of severe persecution, extreme suffering and emotional loss. May our lives be examples of Christ, ever compassionate, full of mercy and ever ready to share the truth of your salvation and your gift of eternal life. Amen

Scripture Application

> NEVER BE LACKING IN ZEAL, BUT KEEP YOUR
> SPIRITUAL FERVOR, SERVING THE LORD.
> BE JOYFUL IN HOPE, PATIENT IN AFFLICTION,
> FAITHFUL IN PRAYER. SHARE WITH
> GOD'S PEOPLE WHO ARE IN NEED.
> PRACTICE HOSPITALITY. BLESS THOSE WHO
> PERSECUTE YOU; BLESS AND DO NOT CURSE.
>
> ROMANS 12: 11- 14

PART THREE

Courage

through

Loss

FOR SINCE DEATH CAME
THROUGH A MAN, THE RESURRECTION
OF THE DEAD COMES ALSO THROUGH A MAN.
FOR AS IN ADAM ALL DIE,
SO IN CHRIST ALL WILL BE MADE ALIVE.
FOR THE PERISHABLE MUST
CLOTHE ITSELF WITH THE IMPERISHABLE,
AND THE MORTAL WITH IMMORTALITY,
THEN THE SAYING THAT IS
WRITTEN WILL COME TRUE:
"DEATH HAS BEEN SWALLOWED UP IN VICTORY."

"WHERE, O DEATH, IS YOUR VICTORY?
WHERE, O DEATH, IS YOUR STING?"
THE STING OF DEATH IS SIN, AND THE
POWER OF SIN IS THE LAW.
BUT THANKS BE TO GOD!
HE GIVES US THE VICTORY THROUGH
OUR LORD JESUS CHRIST.

1 CORINTHIANS 15:21,53-57

Introduction to
Part Three

Courage Through
Loss

Who among us has not felt the sting of death, either from the death of a cherished friend, parent, grandparent or even the unthinkable, the heart-wrenching loss of a child. Most of us cannot fathom the reasoning of death, and its untimely pronouncement on a truly innocent, good person's life. The harsh reality of the pain that comes along with a loved one's death is something we know we must deal with, but just how is that accomplished? How do we grapple with the unseemly demise of a baby, or a young adult's tragic death in the prime of life with much to look forward to and achieve in the world?

It may surprise you to know that our heavenly Father actually grieves the death of his righteous ones and He does not take our deaths lightly. In Psalms 116:15 we read: *Precious in the sight of the Lord is the death of his saints.*

Our Lord understands our pain and suffering and seeks to comfort us when we too must face the moment of leaving this earth and our bodies. I do believe our Lord feels all our sufferings in this world and rejoices when we stand before Him to be with Him for all eternity.

Remember that because of Adam and Eve's disobedience the world and future generations would pay the price through suffering and death. But Eve's ultimate loss, that of her relationship with God, would be restored through the death of Jesus Christ. In 1 Corinthians 15:21 the Apostle Paul put it this way: *For since death came through a man, the resurrection of the dead comes also through a man. For as in Adam all die, so in Christ all will be made alive. For the perishable must clothe itself with the imperishable, and the mortal with immortality, then the saying that is written will come true: "Death has been swallowed up in victory."*

Jesus is the victor over death, so then we too share in this victory! *"Where, O death, is your victory? Where, O death, is your sting?" The sting of death is sin, and the power of sin is the law. But thanks be to God! He gives us the victory through our Lord Jesus Christ.* (1 Corinthians 15:53-57)

It is my hope that through the following true life stories you will see how God's love, grace and strength comforted each woman as she faced the despair of losing a loved one and how He provided courage through loss.

THE OFFICIAL MARTHA WASHINGTON GERANIUM
LOVELY TO BEHOLD, IT HAS IN ITS COUNTENANCE THE HINT OF THE
HAND OF GOD. LIKE MARTHA WASHINGTON IT IS NOT FLASHY OR
PRETENTIOUS BUT SERVES ITS PURPOSE IN THE GARDEN BY DILIGENTLY
AND FAITHFULLY GROWING STRONG ALONGSIDE THE OTHER BLOOMS
THAT ARE NOURISHED BY GOD'S SUNSHINE.

Martha Washington

1731–1802

"Mother" of a Nation

Martha Dandridge was born the oldest daughter of John and Frances Dandridge on June 2, 1731, on a plantation near Williamsburg, Virginia. Her education was for the most part nonexistent, except for the social and domestic skills that were part of every 18th century young girl's life. She did learn the art and skill of maintaining a well-run household and the important aspect of keeping her family happy.

From an early age Martha enjoyed life on the plantation seeking out wildflowers and undiscovered treasures in the fields and nearby woods. Martha, or Patsy, as her family called her, was somewhat of a tomboy who loved the outdoors and to ride her horse, Graylegs, whenever she got the chance. Her mother, Frances, did not approve of her daughter's rambunctious behavior, and if she had her way would have Patsy sit in the parlor as a young lady should, working dutifully on her stitching.

Martha tended to be on the plump side, with fine brown hair and hazel eyes that always seemed to be aglow with an eagerness to embrace life. Her cheeks were in a constant state of blush from being in the outdoors most of the time. Not only did she enjoy riding but she truly loved to care for her flower garden, tending to her tulips and scarlet larkspurs. Papa had seen to it that she had a little plot of land to plant and grow her favorite flowers, giving her many hours of true joy. Her mama, however thought that her husband gave their firstborn too much freedom for such a young lady, and insisted that she practice her lessons on the spinet, or attend to the matters of the home.

Colonel John Dandridge was not only a planter with a large estate, but also clerk of New Kent County, an honorable and lucrative position. The Colonel's brother, William, had married a great-grand niece of the third Lord Delaware and been on the King's Council, and therefore had the right and privilege to display the lion's head coat of arms of the Dandridge's of Great Malvern, Worcestershire, in their native England. All of this had been impressed upon Martha to respect her lineage and to be proud of being a Dandridge.

Martha's three brothers were still being schooled by the time she was fifteen, and her father had hired a new tutor for them, a young man from England. Martha had spent a little time when she was younger learning to read and figure some, but now was forced to spend her time learning to sew for hours on end, and when she wasn't sewing she was learning how to run a household. She almost wished that she could join her brothers as they sat listening to their new tutor from England. But that was only a fleeting thought as she recalled how much she disliked the Primer, with its alphabet all set up in rhymes from A ("Adam's fall/we sinned all.") to Z ("Zaccheus he/Did climb a tree/His Lord to see.") The rhymes had been easy to remember, like the prayers for morning and evening. "Now I lay me down to sleep…" Every night for years she had repeated it. What ever had she been thinking?

Often her brothers and she would ride by the Pamunkey River, enjoying the blossoming trees and shrubs. She especially liked the pink and white dogwoods, and the great masses of rosy pink, creamy white magnolias. It was on one of these rides that she experienced a misadventure that would bring her face to face with her future husband. While riding on the road outside the plantation, Martha's roan, a newly acquired horse, was startled by an approaching rider and she took a fall from the skittish animal. Normally a skillful rider, she was taken aback by her fall from grace and was surprised when she felt strong arms lifting her to her feet. Glancing into his kind, dark eyes, she was warmed by this stranger's genuine concern. He seemed familiar, a slightly handsome man, even though he was probably much older than she, but decidedly younger than her father. But she just could not place this intriguing gentleman, whom she was sure she must know.

Insisting on seeing her home, the kind stranger with the dark eyes escorted Martha and her younger brothers back to the plantation. When her father saw her disheveled state, with mud on her dress and grass and sticks in her hair, he seemed rather perturbed, but before she could barely utter her apology, her father saw her escort.

"Daniel! Daniel Parke Custis!"

Martha was amazed that her father knew her kind guardian and even further surprised to find out that this stranger was her godfather. She had probably been five or six when she last saw him. No wonder he seemed familiar to her, but still a stranger.

It was this brief encounter that led the youthful Martha to ponder this Daniel Custis and his history. Papa told them later that he had never been married and was getting old at thirty-five to still be unattached. She thought on her godfather and decided he was not old at all; at least he didn't look old to her anyway. And he did have a kind twinkle in his eye, didn't he? Yes, he did indeed.

Not more than three years later, in 1849, Martha, now almost eighteen years old and grown in stature and refinement, was waiting by her flower garden while Daniel Parke Custis was asking for her hand in marriage. If papa said yes, they would be married and settle down to a happy home of their own. John Dandridge had given his blessing, but she wasn't counting on her potential father-in-law to refuse to bless their union. Daniel Custis' father was sure there was not a woman on the face of the earth good enough for his son, especially not this New Kent Dandridge girl.

Martha was heartbroken and thought she would never see Daniel again, until another chance meeting with his father changed the course of destiny. Attending the Governor's ball that was held during the spring Assembly in Williamsburg, she chanced by the House of the Six Chimneys, Daniel's father's house, on an afternoon walk with a friend. Seeing the lovely flowers by the road, she stopped to admire them and made small talk with a man she thought to be the gardener.

The "gardener," who was rather rumpled, with powdered wig askew, a shock of red hair defiantly sticking out, was rather taken by this lovely young lady who had sprouted up in his garden. He was very much appreciative of her knowledge of the varied species of flowers in the garden, and offered to give her a tour of the grounds. Never one to miss the opportunity to make a new friend, especially one who could show her an array of flowers, she readily agreed. After a tour of the grounds the two new friends discussed the owner of the beautiful home and property in some detail. Martha remarked that she had heard the master of the grand plantation was a curmudgeon of sorts, but it would be best not to repeat this information. The old gardener stopped in his tracks at this bit of information, but if she had looked beneath the bushy brows she would have seen a twinkle in his eyes as he chuckled to himself.

Of course, as you may have guessed, this gardener was none other than the old curmudgeon himself, Mr. John Custis, Daniel's father. Martha found out that the gardener was really Colonel Custis and was very concerned that he now most certainly would not approve of their marriage, especially after she had called him a curmudgeon!

But Colonel Custis had taken a fancy to the charming young woman who loved not only his flower garden but his son as well. He could now see how easily his son had lost his heart to Martha and why he so eagerly sought her hand in marriage. Martha Dandridge and Daniel Custis became husband and wife in June of 1849, married in St. Peter's Church by Reverend David Mossum, who had been the rector there before Martha had been born. Martha loved St. Peter's with its arched windows, huge tower and steeple that reached out to the peaceful blue skies. The fragrant, pungent air of roses, honeysuckle and laurel called up cherished childhood memories of her hours spent with her family in worship. Her papa owned a pew there and their family worshiped as often as possible, warmly referring to this house of God, as others did, as simply "the Brick Church." This was the center of life for Martha, a life given in morning devotions, giving thanks and worshipping her Savior Jesus Christ. Faith, family and friends would be the foundation on which she would build for the rest of her life.

Not too long after her marriage to Daniel, Martha received news that her beloved brother John, her closest childhood playmate had died, still a boy of seventeen. Martha was glad that they lived only five miles away so she could comfort her mother as she grieved the loss of her firstborn. Tragedy and joy were mingled together as mama tended to the needs of her newest born child, while wiping away the tears shed for her oldest son, an affliction that no mother should ever have to bear.

Martha busied herself with running her household, truly thankful for the instruction that her mother insisted she have on this important aspect of domesticity. Days turned to years and soon happiness was complete when in 1751 Daniel Parke the second entered the Custis home. This little boy was destined to be the apple of his father's eye and he traveled everywhere with his father, sitting before him as his father made rounds on the plantation. A little more than a year later, in April 1753, baby Frances Parke Custis joined her older brother, honoring both grandmothers with her first name.

At the age of forty, Daniel was a doting father who could not do enough for his offspring. He was always ordering the latest in toys, trinkets and fineries with every ship that set sail with his fine tobacco to London. He loved to lavish his son, daughter and beloved wife with all that life had to offer in the 16th century, his love knowing no bounds.

Then the unthinkable happened to the happy family when little Daniel became ill while out riding with his father. The two-and-a-half-year-old had contracted what Martha believed was one of his many colds, so she took many measures to help overcome his fever and cough. Daniel blamed himself for taking the boy out in the cold, even though his wife tried to reassure him that he could not have known that it was going to snow so hard. She tried to remain calm in the situation believing that this cold would surely break before long and their once sturdy son would be up and running about in no time. But he only proceeded to fall further into his illness, finally alarming Martha into sending for the doctor. The doctor tried all the conventional methods of the time, blood letting, leeches and the scalding mustard plasters that she hated so much (hated seeing them on her son's tender, smooth skin). But it was all to no avail, and little Daniel breathed his last and shattered his father's resolve that he should live. Though Martha was devastated with grief, she felt even more pain for her husband who seemed to age overnight. The loss of his son was more than he could physically bear, blaming himself for his death, thinking if only he hadn't taken him riding that day.

Daniel Custis turned his all-consuming devotion to baby Frances, focusing all his love and attention on her, checking on her during the day, interrupting his care and management of the fields. When John Parkes Custis came into the world, Martha could not have been happier; not only for herself, but for her husband. Daniel soon seemed like himself again and the days were marked with sowing and reaping, holidays and parties, life at its best, life being lived to the fullest. In 1755 another child was born, a girl whom Daniel insisted should be named Martha, but called Patsy, of course. Baby Patsy was delicate and very beautiful, and her mother was content that she had been born a girl, a secret desire that she had kept to herself.

Since the passing of Colonel Custis some years before, Martha and Daniel had taken to staying at the House of Six Chimneys in Williamsburg for the Assembly. It seemed strange for her to be the mistress of the grand mansion and its beautiful grounds, the grounds where she had unknowingly called her future father-in-law a curmudgeon. But she had planted a little yew tree there in the garden, so it began to seem more and more like her own.

Between preparing for the Governor's Ball and all the other gala activities, dinners and dances, there was much talk about the troops that were continuing to push the ever advancing French back into their territory. One such promising hero was a young Virginian who was leading expeditions, building forts and defending His Majesty's colonies against the encroaching French in the western territories. Such talk was nearly heard all the time, and the names most associated with this talk were Braddock, Monongahela and Lieutenant Colonel George Washington, the young Virginian. Rumors began spreading that Colonel Washington was in Williamsburg! Then there were the reports of his dying or even that he was most certainly dead. When, on the morning of August 27, Colonel Washington did arrive in Williamsburg, the whole town rallied to see if they could catch a glimpse of the handsome young militiaman.

Martha had been out walking with her sister Nancy and a few others when a group of burgesses passed by in their powdered wigs, velvet coats and breeches, looking very official and important. Then all of a sudden her sister clutched her arm and exclaimed, "Look there he is! Colonel Washington! The tall one!"

Yes, he was tall and was rather plainly dressed in his blue uniform with red facings of the Virginia militia, contrasting oddly with the elaborately bedecked burgesses. His hair was only slightly powdered, and Martha was glad that he wasn't too caught up in appearances like the pretentious officials. Martha looked into his eyes and thought the grey-blue eyes were kind but seemed very tired. He was also pale and looked like he was probably very sick. Nancy thought he was the handsomest man she had ever seen and Martha half jokingly asked her if she would like to be married to the eligible Colonel. Her sister only laughed and said she thought him too stern, with his lips drawn together so thin and unsmiling. Martha had not thought so, rather waging that he was more worried, weary and perhaps even in some pain. After all, he had been in the middle of war, so that was only to be expected. But no sooner had he arrived in town than he was gone, back into the unknown territories tracking the French and Indians.

With life moving ever forward in cycles, once again the good merged into the bad, as all life was want to do, ebbing and flowing as the river that clutched the banks near her parental home. Her dear papa was ill, and she was summoned to Chestnut Grove immediately as the doctor feared he only had hours to live. Daniel and Martha made their way to her father's bedside in the nick of time. As she knelt beside him, his eyes sparkled with what little life still lingered within at the sight of his daughter. Her heart was breaking, so much death so close together, too much too soon. How must she bear all the anguish? Must life continue to press such pain on her and her loved ones? Not only one loss, but now three! Her beloved brother, her little boy, and now her very own father! What would her mother do? She had a new baby at her breast, little Mary, born in April, just four months before this tragedy. Poor little Mary would never know how wonderful her papa truly was, but she promised to make sure that she would grow up knowing and never forgetting her father.

Martha took heart in the steady rhythm of the seasons and weighed each day with the enormity of the tasks at hand. Like clockwork they attended the assembly each year, making the rounds of dinners, balls and dances. They also toiled the land, harvesting the tobacco crops, shipping their bounty to England and seeing to their household and other duties. Worship was always at the beginning of the day and Martha spent an hour of devotion every morning in the Holy Scriptures.

It was on one such morning that Daniel decided to take little Frances for a ride with him, her bright eyes sparkling in eager anticipation. The two happily went out into the March air as Martha retired to her room to pray and read the Psalms, Psalms of thanksgiving and joy. But soon her joy took a turn of alarm as her husband bounded back through the door with his daughter in his arms, cheeks blazing red, her skin unnaturally hot.

Martha gathered her trembling, small body in her arms and scanned her face with mother's eyes filled with anxious concern. She chided herself and guilt permeated her heart and mind; why hadn't she been more cautious, why did she allow her daughter to ride when she was obviously ill? It was another nightmare, just as it had been for her son, now her daughter was suffering in much the same way. Daniel quickly sent for the doctor through one of his servants, sent on the fastest horse that he owned, determined to find aid for their daughter as she slipped further away from them with each movement of the hands of the clock. Laying cool clothes on her child's body, Martha administered quinine, lobelia, and calomel for her increasing fever, using all the remedies she knew to try to relieve the persistent fever.

When the doctor arrived he used all the same treatments that had been used on little Daniel as he lay dying. The same leeches administered to the pale little body, the same blood letting through cuts in the tiny veins, all to no avail. Just as it had been for her boy, the end came in the morning, with the birds calling out to the newly arriving day, heralding the freshness of life, all the while death sped through the bedroom window of the anguished little family. Finally the tortured small body became still, her flushed, feverish cheeks now pale and her once bright eyes fixed, forever frozen in time. Her mother closed the eyes and drew the coverlet over the pale face, knowing she would never gaze on her beautiful daughter's face ever again.

Once more death had knocked on the Custis' door, and Martha wished that she had not had to answer this sinister visitor's call once again. Her heart was broken and forlorn. How could she ever face life with all of this sorrow crowding her soul and her mind? But she knew she must, for life had to be lived on its terms, not her own, and she knew she would seek comfort from the scriptures as she had in times past. Her grief must wait, mostly because she feared for Daniel's well-being. She knew he would blame himself once again, because this disaster was too much like the previous one—taking his young daughter out riding—just as he had done with little Daniel. The burden on her was to reassure her husband that it had not been the ride; it had been a beautiful, warm day, and he had given his daughter one last happy experience with her father before she succumbed to the illness that would claim her young life. But he would not be consoled, and it seemed to his worried wife that he had aged at least ten years since the moment Frances had died. The trauma of the loss of both his children took a lasting toll on Daniel and he would never recover from the emotional onslaught of his heart.

Martha not only worried about the change in Daniel since Frances' death, there was also the pallor that clung to his face, and then there was the persistent cough that would not ease. Something was not quite right. Even though he continued to ride throughout the plantation each morning he seemed so weary and out of breath he often had to return home to rest and try and recover. His weight loss was significant, so Martha tried to tempt him with a variety of foods, even concocting herbal remedies in an effort to help his failing energy. She fought her own despondency in an effort to encourage him with her cheerfulness and happy countenance, but to her discouragement, none of these efforts worked to change his decrease in health. Daniel tried to rally his strength and resolve, even traveling to

Williamsburg to seek out a physician that was a well-known apothecary in Virginia. Perhaps this doctor would be able to help him, and on his return he assured Martha that the physician told him that time would resolve all of these problems. It had not been a deception really, the doctor had said time would take care of the persistent illness, but actually he had told Daniel that he did not have long to live.

Then on July 4 Daniel fell very ill and took to his bed. Dr. Carter was sent for immediately through a messenger to Williamsburg, and when he arrived on the fifth he promised Martha that he would stay as long as he was needed. She would not leave her husband's bedside, waiting patiently for his weakened arms to envelop her and kiss her fears away. She knew he wanted her there, so there she remained until she lost all awareness of time. Holding his hand, touching what little warmness was left gave her reassurance that just maybe her loving, kind, gentle, protective husband would return to her. How could she lose him too? How would she survive this madness, hadn't she endured enough with all of these losses? Brother, father, son, daughter, and now husband. Perhaps she thought, *Please God, might you spare my husband?* But on July 8, 1757, Daniel Parke Custis slipped away into eternal life at age 45.

Mama would be the one Martha would turn to now, mama who had lost a husband and who had a little girl as well to raise alone. How could she face life again, how could she possibly go forward to face such a bleak future alone? She had rested on Daniel for everything, for assurance, protection and security. Sometimes she resented his treating her like a child, but now she realized she really had been one in the beginning of their marriage, but now through adversity and tragedy she was forced to be wise beyond her years.

Frances Dandridge was a comfort to her daughter, understanding and even practical in the face of uncertainty. "You must go on. You are young, only twenty-six, with young children who are depending on your guidance. Patsy, time will heal your pain, you will see, eventually you will find life worth living again."

Turning as always to her morning devotions Martha found little comfort in the reading of scripture as she once had. The Psalms that had proclaimed thanksgiving and joy a short time before just did not ring true in her life. Life had ended for her, of that she was sure, never to be enjoyed again.

What the young widow and single mother could not guess at this moment of her darkest hour was that she was going to go down in history as the "Mother of our Nation." Through her kind friends and neighbors, the Chamberlaynes, she would reacquaint herself with the charming Colonel Washington, the tall, kind man that all Virginia seemed to gravitate to and admire. Washington soon proposed marriage, and they married on January 6, 1759, leaving her estate and moving to his plantation, Mount Vernon, on the Potomoc. Her children lovingly regarded him as "father" and Martha even asked if George would like to adopt them, but in his heart he thought it only right that they remain Custis to honor their father Daniel. He knew that he would love them as his own, and they him without the formality of an adoption.

George would become the stability and one constant source of happiness and pride in Martha's life. He wanted to take care of "Patsy," as he came to call her, and she wanted nothing more than to take care of her husband, making sure he was well fed and healthy. It was her nature and calling to be a doting wife and mother, and she resolved that her family would always come first in everything.

Patsy regarded George Washington's reputation as a hero with respect and honor, acknowledging his preeminent standing among his peers, but to her he was "her husband." They lived as husband and wife for forty years through accolades, presidential appointment, family illness and hardships. They were committed to each other first and foremost, and when he succumbed to death in December of 1799, Martha knew she would soon follow her beloved.

It was May, the most beautiful month at Mount Vernon, the lilacs and apple trees in bloom, the gardens bursting with spring color. Martha was ill, lying in her bed with the windows thrown open. She felt the warm air as it stirred the fresh bouquet of lilacs that her granddaughter had brought up to her third floor bedroom to cheer her. She wasn't sure what all the fuss was about, since she was at peace, a feeling of well-being enveloping her in spite of the insipid heat that assaulted her body.

It was odd how everyone was creeping about in quiet tones and muted conversations. She could recognize their faces, but noticed George was not among them, perhaps he was away on a trip somewhere. Cheerfully she talked with them, sharing her Christian faith in encouragement and all of the divine promises of the Bible that she had read her whole life. It seemed strange when everything started to blur and then there was a kind, gentle man placing a piece of bread in her mouth, a goblet of wine pressed to her lips. Where was she? St. Peters? No, that could not be right she hadn't been there in so very many years. She must be in Church though…receiving the sacraments, but no, there was Dr. Davis looking at her, so she could not be in church. No, she was in her own bedroom in the garret. Where was George? Surely he should be here with her after all. Oh, she thought, he was waiting for her to come to him, so she must pack and get ready. My goodness, there was so much to do, with gathering clothes, food and ordering the chariot and horses. At last, everything was ready and George was waiting for her, yes it was time to go, everything was in order and prepared.

The Washington Federalist paper reported "on Saturday evening, the 22nd , widow of the late illustrious General George Washington. To those amiable and Christian virtues, which adorn the female character, she added dignity of manners, superiority of understanding, a mind intelligent and elevated. The silence of respectful grief is our best eulogy."

Martha Dandridge Custis Washington never considered herself educated, intelligent, or even a patriot. But what she did understand was loyalty to God, family and her convictions. Martha Washington was indeed a woman of courage and faith.

Scripture Application

I WILL PRAISE THE LORD WHO COUNSELS ME;
EVEN AT NIGHT MY HEART INSTRUCTS ME.
I HAVE SET THE LORD ALWAYS BEFORE ME.
BECAUSE HE IS AT MY RIGHT HAND,
I WILL NOT BE SHAKEN.

PSALM 16:7-9

OKLAHOMA TEXAS MIX
RED, GOLD, BLUE AND WHITE FLOWERS IN THIS MIX DISPLAY INTENSE
VIBRANCY. SEEMINGLY GROWING FREE AT FIRST BLUSH, IT BECOMES
APPARENT THAT THE FLOWERS ARE SUSTAINED AND FLOURISHING
THANKS TO THE MASTER GARDENER. DALE EVANS' LIFE WAS IMBUED IN
JUST THIS WAY, UPHELD IN THE STRONG ARMS OF HER SAVIOR.

Dale Evans Rogers

1912 - 2001

Queen of the West

Dale Evans Rogers was born Frances Octavia Smith in Uvalde, Texas, in her grandparents' house to Walter Smith and Betty Sue Hillman Smith on October 31, 1912. Walter was a farmer and owner of a hardware store in the small town of Italy, Texas, population 1,000. A formal birth certificate was not issued to her parents, so they signed an affidavit stating that she indeed was born in Uvalde, Texas, on October 31, 1912, and her name was Frances Octavia Smith.

Little Frances showed musical talent even at the mere age of three when she made her singing debut at the baptist church in her home town of Italy. It was her solo rendition of a Gospel song that became her first ever performance. In 1919 when she was seven years old her father uprooted the family to make the move to the town of Osceola, Arkansas, in Mississippi County after his brother assured him of the bountiful cotton crops that were raised there. Unfortunately he failed to disclose the abundance of boll weevils, mosquitoes and devastating floods. She and her brother Hillman suffered along with her parents through that miserable first year that didn't live up to the promises her uncle made for their prosperity and joy. It was nothing like the picture he had so illustriously painted for the eager young Smith family. The next year proved to be much better in all respects, so her uncle was out of the dog house, so to speak.

Mother Betty Sue was her children's teacher in all the areas of basic learning—reading, writing and arithmetic—but by the time Frances was seven she was registered to begin school in Osceola, beginning in the first grade. She excelled in her lessons and so she only spent a half a year there and was promoted to the third grade. Keeping up with her studies seemed relatively easy, but when they advanced her to the eighth grade when she was only eleven years old, the difficulty in matching the older kids' work proved too much. She faltered in both her studies and her emotions, resulting in her doctor ordering her to spend the summer resting in bed. Even then though, she took piano lessons, frustrating her instructor by her stubborn refusal to practice her scales. Eventually the teacher quit when Frances insisted on composing and improvising her own songs.

Seemingly stubborn and emotional, Frances always wanted her way. At age 14 she met a much older boy at a public dance, and they impulsively eloped to nearby Blytheville (Mississippi County). Frances Octavia Smith and Thomas Fox made their way to the home of a local minister where they lied about their ages and were officially married. The very young couple decided to start out on their own, moving to Memphis, Tennessee, where later that year their son, Thomas Fox Jr. was born. Thomas realized not too long after that they had made a terrible mistake.

He decided that he was much too young to be tied down to a wife and child, so at the tender age of seventeen, Francis became a divorcee with a young child.

Realizing that her little boy had no one to depend on but her, she took courses at a business school, working as a secretary while aspiring to become a singer. While working at a bus company she began to look for a higher paying job and found one at a Memphis insurance company. One day her boss overheard her singing at her desk and was inspired to help his employee find work as a singer on WMC and WREC radio stations' programs that were sponsored by the insurance company. It wasn't long before Frances Octavia Smith Fox became a regular fixture on the radio show singing and playing the piano, working under the names Frances Fox and Marian Lee.

In 1930, she decided to move to Chicago with her son Tommy to pursue her singing career in a larger radio market. While looking for work she became ill and was diagnosed with acute malnutrition, which put her quest for employment on hold while she gained strength and recovered. As soon as she was able, she began the job search once again, this time moving to Louisville, Kentucky, where her luck was much better. Not only did she land a radio job at WHAS, she finally secured the name that she would be known by for the rest of her life, Dale Evans. Joe Eaton, station manager at the time, renamed her Dale Evans because he thought it easier for radio announcers to pronounce, and it rolled easier off the tongue than Frances Fox. She thought the name was too much of a boy's name and protested a bit, but Joe won out, saying the name was trendy. Perhaps it was his story about a beautiful actress of the silent film era that helped change her mind. The actress' name was Dale Winter and he admired her so much that he wanted to name his new protégé after her in respect and honor.

Dale Evans gained much popularity as an on air personality, singing and playing piano, eventually moving into the clubs in the Louisville area. When her son Tommy became sick she decided to move back home to her parents' farm in Italy, Texas (they had since moved back form Arkansas), where her parents could look after her son. She was able to find work in several clubs in Texas and found work in Dallas at station WFAA, spending weekends with her family. While working in Dallas, Dale heard from Robert Dale Butts, a pianist and orchestra leader she had known in Louisville. When he was able to make the move to Dallas and secure a job at the same station as she, they decided to marry.

Their new life together began in 1937, and the couple agreed to make the move to Chicago, leaving Tommy with her parents, while they sought work. Tommy found work right off the bat at the local NBC radio affiliate, and Dale found several singing jobs with big bands. What might have been the greatest break in the singer's career happened when she was offered the opportunity to tour with the Anson Weeks Orchestra. She happily accepted and began a cross-country tour that lasted an entire year, including an eight-week stint in sunny California, Los Angeles to be exact. While there she naturally scouted the area for possible jobs for the future. Disappointed, she returned home with the orchestra and her husband to Chicago. Once home she began work at radio station WBBM, the local CBS affiliate where talent scouts from Paramount discovered her and arranged a screen test for her in Hollywood with dancing legend Fred Astaire. Dale was quick to respond. While she did not garner the role in the movie *Holiday Inn* (released in 1942) with Bing Crosby and Fred Astaire, she did secure the role of client with Hollywood agent Joe Rivkin. A few details of her life were changed when she signed with Joe to represent her—he made her "seven years younger" and made her son, Tommy, into her brother.

When Joe gave her screen test to Twentieth Century Fox, she was signed to a one-year contract to star in several films for them, *Orchestra Wives* and *Girl Trouble*, all in 1942. This exposure helped Dale to secure a contract with the top ranked Chase and Sanborn Show, which was broadcast nationwide. She had the pleasure of joining the likes of Don Ameche, Jimmy Durante, Edgar Bergen (Candace Bergen's father) and of course Charlie McCarthy (Bergen's ventriloquist dummy). There were always a mix of big stars to share the spotlight with and the programs looked like a list of Hollywood's who's who. She also performed for the military through a USO Troupe in World War II, sharing her love of entertaining with those that were facing the horrors and loneliness of war.

Republic Studios became interested in Dale and signed her to a one-picture contract with a one-year option. The picture was *Swing Your Partner,* and after this film the option was used to cast her in a variety of contemporary movies, including a John Wayne western where she had the chance to sing.

Republic's biggest star at the time was Roy Rogers. Herbert Yates, head of Republic Studios, was inspired by the successful stage play *Oklahoma* and wanted to expand the female lead in his westerns. Using this formula he speculated that he could make Roy Rogers an even bigger name in the movie industry and was looking for the right leading lady to complement his star. Dale Evans, he reasoned, had a large following and quite a reputation as a singer, plus she was from Texas and must know a thing or two about "riden' 'n ropen." With this subjugated reasoning he was right on the money concerning his new female lead's vocal talent, but her skills as a cowgirl left a lot to be desired. No matter, destiny was meant to be fulfilled, and Herbert Yates cast Dale in *The Cowboy and the Senorita,* released in 1944—the first of 28 films that Dale and Roy would make together.

Roy had become a widower when his first wife, Arlene Wilkins Rogers, died in 1946, leaving him to raise their three children (Cheryl, Linda Lou and Dusty) alone. Dale had been divorced from Robert Butts in 1945. Working so closely with Roy as her leading man, sparks just naturally began to fly. They proved to be a popular pair with their fans and continued to co-star in such films as *Yellow Rose of Texas* (1944), *Lights of Old Santa Fe* (1944) and *Utah* (1945). The acting team of Rogers and Evans was officially an on-screen success, yet off-screen their lives were just beginning to rival that success. But this was not play-acting, this was for real.

Roy Rogers and Dale Evans were married on December 31, 1947 at the Flying L. Ranch near Davis, Oklahoma, where they had just completed filming *Home in Oklahoma*. Eventually, as a new family, the couple revealed that Dale's son Tom was not her brother as reported, but truly her son who was now 20 years old.

Together the couple had a daughter, Robin Elizabeth, who was born on August 26, 1950 when Dale was 37 years old. Dale had not been well during her pregnancy, even coming down with a mild case of German measles. Medical science had not yet realized the threat that German measles poses for unborn children, and since Dale hadn't felt very sick, she had no idea what her illness could mean for her baby. Soon after their daughter was born the doctors broke the news to them about baby Robin's disability, Down's Syndrome. Not much was known about Down's Syndrome in those days, except that it had been recognized for centuries with no known reason for its cause. At that time it was called "mongolism," and it was given that name because of the slanted eyes that are characteristic of a Down's baby. There were other problems that were characteristic of Down's Syndrome, a thicker tongue, a weaker cry, poor muscle tone, a heart murmur, developmental disabilities and mental retardation.

Robin Elizabeth Rogers was a special, delicate flower born at a time when even doctors could see no clear reason for the worth of a severely disabled child. Robin was born at a time when people struggled with the human worth and value in a person who did not appear "normal." Doctors at the time strongly advised Dale and Roy to institutionalize their baby girl and get on with their lives. But they determined to bring Robin home, where she belonged, with her family. They believed that God had sent her to their family for a special reason, and that they had no right to cast her away. For whatever reason, the sovereign Lord of life had chosen them to love and nurture this precious flower. Dale and her family loved the short time with their little one. When she would smile or laugh it would light up the world for all of them.

The older children had come down with the mumps, and even though Robin and her nurse stayed quietly away from the other children, she came down with them as well, a week before her second birthday. As her brothers and sisters recovered normally, she fought bravely as her temperature climbed to 108 degrees. The doctor told Dale that Robin had mumps encephalitis. If she recovered, she would suffer severe brain damage. On Saturday, Baby Robin had been screaming in pain for almost a week from the brain infection. By Sunday morning, the screaming had stopped. Robin had slipped into unconsciousness and by late afternoon time seemed to have come to a stand still.

Dale and Roy were saddened beyond words and when they buried their little girl on her birthday, they thought their tears would never end. Dale explained Robin's death to her children by telling them that she had gone to heaven to be with Jesus, and that she was happy there and would never have any more pain. The children were happy that Robin wasn't in pain any more, but they missed "their" baby. By summer's end Dale's hair turned completely white.

Dale decided to write a book about her baby daughter's short life with them. *Angel Unaware* honored their baby, who had brought life and sunshine into their lives. As a way of helping others, she designated all of the royalties to go to the National Association for Retarded Children. Today that book is in its twenty-eighth printing. It has comforted thousands of families with children like Robin, and it has challenged the world to be more compassionate.

Dale's Christian faith helped her cope with her daughter's death and prepared her to handle the many tragedies that would strike their family. The couple became foster and adoptive parents to other special needs children—Dodie, Marion, and Deborah Lee. Debbie died at age 12 in a tragic bus accident while on a church outing. Debbie had begged to go on this trip to Tijuana, Mexico, to take gifts to the children in an orphanage. Because her birthday was coming up she knew her mom would probably say yes because she always let the kids chose something special for their birthday. Dale could not bring herself to say no to that upturned face and happy smile, so she hugged her daughter and agreed that she could make the trip.

When she heard of Debbie's violent death, Dale burst into uncontrollable tears, collapsing against a window seat in her house, crying, "Why God? Why did you do this to me again? Why my baby again? Oh Jesus please, please help me!"

Dusty, her son, sat down with her and took her by the shoulders, giving her a little shake to get her attention. "Mom!"

he said firmly. "Mom! For as long as I can remember, you've been telling me to trust Jesus. Now is the time for you to do that! Debbie is okay! She's with Him!" She nodded and put her head in his lap and cried. She lay there comforted by her son for what seemed like hours and wondered how she would tell Roy, who was in the hospital recovering from back surgery.

Another tragedy struck when their son John David (Sandy) died as a result of drinking with some of his G.I. buddies while stationed in Germany. Sandy was only eighteen years old at the time, and was not known to be a big drinker, only having a beer from time to time. The soldiers had just completed maneuvers and to celebrate they decided to throw a bash. Sandy just wanted to fit in—to belong—and so he just went along with the crowd. Sandy consumed an enormous amount of alcohol that night, all to prove that he was a man and that he fit in with the other guys. All of this alcohol was too overwhelming for his stomach and system, and he began to vomit. One of Sandy's buddies took him to the infirmary, where the doctors checked on him several times during the night. At 2 a.m. he seemed to be all right, and again at 3 he responded to the doctor, but sometime between 3 and 6 a.m. he must have choked to death.

Roy, Dusty, and the other children had received the devastating news about Sandy before Dale, who was flying home that night from a trip to Texas. To make matters worse, it was her birthday. When they all went to the airport to meet the plane, Roy heartbreakingly asked his pastor Bill Hanson, "How am I ever going to tell her?"

"Do you want me to?"

Roy shook his head. "No I'll take care of it."

But no one had to say a word. The minute she saw her family standing there she knew and cried out "Oh, my God, not Sandy! Not Sandy! He's in Germany, not Viet Nam!"

Suddenly her legs went out from under her, and Roy grabbed her. A couple of security men rushed over, and helped her and the family into a small private room. Dale was hysterical for over two hours.

The military funeral was held at Forest Lawn Cemetery and Sandy was buried next to his sisters, Debbie and Robin. Dale and her family knew it wasn't Sandy that was being lowered into the cold, dark ground. They knew without a doubt that Sandy was with God.

In remembrance of her children Dale wrote the book, *Dearest Debbie and Salute to Sandy*. Dale was a gifted writer, both in song and in book form, writing some 25 songs, including "Happy Trails," which became the couple's theme song. Dale had written the lyrics on an envelope minutes before their radio show and taught Rogers and the singing group, Sons of the Pioneers, the melody. The other big musical hit she had was her inspirational piece, "The Bible Tells Me So." Her books, 17 in all, dealt primarily with her faith and how she and her family dealt with the tragic loss of their children. She also worked tirelessly as a lay minister, counseling others who suffered losses as well and volunteered as often as she was asked, always thinking of others who were in pain.

Roy and Dale founded their own production company, Roy Rogers Productions and created "The Roy Rogers Show" (1951-1957), "The Roy Rogers and Dale Evans Show" (1962) and Happy Trails Theatre (1986-89). There was even a television special called "Saga of Sonora" in 1973 that proved very popular for a generation of devoted fans. Then there were the restaurants that Roy successfully licensed his name to in order, the creators of the chain hoped, to promote the all-American fare that his hungry fans would consume. They must have liked the food because at the restaurant's peak there were more than 600 across the nation, many of which hosted personal appearances by Evans and Rogers.

Dale has received many honors including the California Mother of the Year Award (1967) The Texas Press Association's Texan of the Year (1970), Cardinal Terrance Cook Humanities Award (1995) and her induction into the Cowgirl Hall of Fame. Not only did she receive these wonderful awards, but she has three stars on The Hollywood Walk of Fame as well.

Retirement seemed to be rather elusive for Dale as she entered those golden years of life, and instead of slowing down, she became the host of her own weekly program on the Christian television network, TBN, called "A Date With Dale," holding interviews and offering encouragement to her vast audience. This program was broadcast worldwide and translated into many languages, just as her movies with Roy had been. Roy Rogers and Dale Evans movies and television programs are sure to be seen playing at any given moment somewhere in the world. With limited engagements, Dale continued as a best-selling author and seemed to always have at least one book in the process of publication. The Roy Rogers-Dale Evans Museum in Victorville, California, where the two often made appearances, houses their many years of memorabilia and chronicles their lives in film, as well as their Christian values and faith.

Through their 50 years of marriage, Dale and Roy had experienced much joy and heart ache, but they remained together, committed to each other and to the family they cherished through their love and the love of God. Roy died from heart failure in 1998, and she passed away on February 7, 2001, from the same condition.

Dale and Roy are buried at Sunset Hill Memorial Park in Apple Valley, California, their memorial stones inscribed with their birth names, Leonard Franklin Slye and Frances Octavia Smith. Of course we will always remember our favorite King and Queen of The West as Roy Rogers and Dale Evans. Upon Dale's passing her survivors included six children, sixteen grandchildren, thirty-two great-grandchildren and six great-great-grandchildren.

Dale Evans and Roy Rogers established the Happy Trails Foundation for abused children that, in turn, hosts the annual Roy Rogers-Dale Evans Western Film Festival that began in 1998 near their former ranch in California. Their legacy remains with us in their charitable gifts and film, something that we all will remember, at least for our lifetime if not longer through future cowboys and cowgirls.

As a long time fan of Miss Rogers and her loving husband Roy, all I can say is "Happy Trails to You…until we meet again."

Scripture Application

REMEMBER YOUR WORD TO
YOUR SERVANT, FOR YOU
HAVE GIVEN ME HOPE.
MY COMFORT IN MY SUFFERING
IS THIS: YOUR PROMISE
PRESERVES MY LIFE.

PSALM 119:49-50

SHOUT FOR JOY TO THE LORD,
ALL THE EARTH. WORSHIP
THE LORD WITH GLADNESS;
COME BEFORE HIM WITH
JOYFUL SONGS.

PSALM 100:1-2

ROSE CALLA LILLIES

Beautiful and elegant, this flower grows gracefully,
knowing the loving care of the Tender Gardner who says,
"Be still, remain in Me." Elizabeth Prentiss drew all her strength
from abiding in the Lord. In her abiding, she also glorified
God and strengthened others through her writing.

Elizabeth Payson Prentiss

1818–1879

Mother, Author, Consoler

Elizabeth Prentiss was born the fifth child of eight children to Reverend and Mrs. Edward Payson of Portland, Maine. Edward Payson was a renowned preacher and a dynamic man of God who instilled in his young daughter the love and power that only comes through Jesus Christ. Like her father, Elizabeth struggled and fought valiantly her entire life with severe, never-ending physical illness and suffering. This thorn in the flesh brought her into a wonderful place of insight into the blessedness of trials that face God's own. Through her afflictions she was able to minister to others in her life and the world through prolific writings.

When Elizabeth was just a child, she entered her father's study to find him prostrate on the floor, lost in prayer. The remembrance of this scene penetrated her heart and mind, and she never forgot the sight. Her love for her father knew no bounds, and it was with the same affection that he loved her. Commenting on her birth in a letter to his parents he stated, "Still God is kind to us. Louisa and the babe continue as well as we could desire. I can still scarcely help thinking that God is preparing me for some severe trial, but if He will grant me His presence as he does now, no trial can seem severe."

It was as if this blessing, this gift from God was almost too good to be true. With such a beautiful baby girl to behold in life, surely something was going to happen to upset such a complete joy! But the resolve to stand strong no matter the offense was embedded deeply in Edward Payson and nothing could sway or discourage him from giving all praise to his heavenly Father. This was the legacy he left to his baby daughter, a legacy of joy and contentment, to rest ever so sweetly in the presence of God.

Elizabeth's disposition and character was one of sunny enthusiasm and bright joy and in conjunction with her deep abiding sympathy for all who were afflicted, we can see a more complete picture of this precious child of God. It is a picture of a lovely flower shining and reaching upwards in the sun, a flower bravely rooted in deep soil, able to withstand the fiercest storms that attempt to uproot and devastate. It is the picture of a woman that left an indelible impression on her family and on the world.

When Edward Payson succumbed to the severe illness that had plagued him for so many years, he was only 45 years old. Little Elizabeth, who was only nine years of age, decided to set in her mind all the details of his life during those last months. She wanted to cherish those memories the way she cherished her father, capturing the moments as a vivid recollection that would surround her for the rest of her life.

Upon finding herself a new widow, Louisa Prentiss was at a loss as to what to do, until her eldest daughter of eighteen, also named Louisa, determined that she would open up a girls' school in New York City. So Mrs. Payson gathered up her brood of children and they all relocated to the City. It was during the one year that they spent there that Elizabeth, a slender, dark-eyed child of twelve, thoughtful and intelligent beyond her years, joined the Presbyterian Church. Within time, Mrs. Payson decided to establish and run a second school in Portland while Louisa continued running the New York school.

In 1832 the doors were open to the Portland school with much success and significance due to Mrs. Payson's wise management of both schools. Through her strength of character, her active mind, warm heart, and practical economic skill, she was able to aid her daughter in the day to day running of the NY school while being an administrator in the Portland school.

Louisa was gifted with astounding knowledge, being an earnest student of Greek, Hebrew and Latin, as well as metaphysics and theology. Indeed her intelligence and university level knowledge helped her to be a most graceful and pertinent writer and because of that she was able to begin a lengthy career of teaching in exchange for which the school published her writing. Louisa eventually married Professor Hopkins of Williamstown and could have easily risen to astounding heights among the American literary contingency, but due to her rapidly declining health, she instead retreated to a more peaceful place in life.

Within the ebb and flow of daily life at the school, Elizabeth was one of her sister's most promising students. "Lizzy," at the age of sixteen was the grateful occupant of a "snuggery" of her own, a certain "Blue Room" assigned her by her mother who best understood her love of quiet hours for meditation and writing. Her father's desk was hers now, and on it she penned, at the suggestion of Mr. Nathaniel Willis, short stories and verses for the "Youth's Companion." This proliferate work came about over a course of twenty years and eventually came into its own as a little volume titled, *Only a Dandelion*.

Elizabeth at nineteen was somewhat shy and withdrawn, spending most of her time in the "Blue Room," in quiet and thoughtful reverie. She was much better at writing than speaking with others, so the blank page became a friend that she eagerly sought out, hoping to convey her longings and intense fluttering of imagination. Truly a young, educated, New England woman of her day was expected to do more with her life than fritter it away on "thoughts" of no particular consequence. She knew that her family expected her to use her knowledge to become an educator of willing minds. So to the resolve of others, she settled on teaching as her future profession.

But it was apparent that God had other ideas for the young and impressionable woman. In the twenty-first year of Elizabeth's life, there came an epoch in her spiritual history that would color her life forevermore. For some unknown reason she was convinced that she had committed the unforgivable sin of rejecting the Holy Spirit. The crushing blow of possibly grieving away the wooing of the Spirit caused her to sink into a deep and perplexing anguish. The pang of her supposed rejection rang throughout her being and brought such deep angst that she supposed the holy, just wrath of the Father was going to consume her with fire. Had her dear father been alive, he would have sympathized with her fear and would have been able to reassure her that God was not deaf and most certainly understood her self-imposed guilt. He would have comforted her, bringing her back into the knowledge of the forgiveness and love of the Father for his earthly children.

Years later her husband described this dark page of her life this way: "The indications are very plain that her morbidly-sensitive, melancholy temperament had much to do with this experience. Her account of it shows, also, that her mind was unhappily affected by certain false notions of the Christian life and ordinances then, and still, more or less prevalent—notions based upon a too narrow and legal conception of the Gospel."

In a letter to a favorite cousin she wrote, "...to direct me over and over again to go with difficulties and temptations and sin to the Savior. I love to be led there and left there. Sometimes when the 'exceeding sinfulness of sin' becomes painfully apparent, there is nothing for the soul to do but to lie in the dust before God without a word of excuse; and that feeling of abasement in His sight is worth more that all the pleasures in the world."

Elizabeth's blessing of being pulled out of "self" came with the invitation to teach in Mr. Persico's seminary for girls in Richmond, Virginia. Soon upon her accepting the principal's offer, Elizabeth began to feel the pull of that stern discipline of her inner character and disposition that aided her ability to focus her attention on the tasks at hand, rather than introspective melancholy renderings. With less time for dreamy introspection she grew stronger and happier daily, even in spite of homesickness and having to be around people so much of the time.

However, in her letters the occasional moribund feelings were expressed to those closest to her. To one correspondent she confessed that she suffered "excruciating pain" from what some doctors pronounced to be angina pectoris. To another friend she said that the warm weather made her "feel as if she were in an oven with hot melted lead poured over her brain." In another letter she mentions her "encouragement in reading my father's memoir, in reflecting that he passed through greater conflicts than will probably ever be mine." This same journal and many letters were saved from destruction through her husband's watchful diligence. It speaks volumes of the struggles and the triumphs of this brave and growing inner woman over weariness, loneliness and afflictions.

Mr. Persico was so impressed with Elizabeth's teaching in that very first year that he sent her an urgent recall in November of 1842 to return for a second year. But upon her return for the second session she was dismayed to find that the administration had changed and her experience was far less pleasant than before. Mr. Persico had lost heart after his wife's death and could not pay his teachers their salary nor pay his debtors. Elizabeth determined to stay amidst personal financial loss and mental exhaustion until the dreary summer term closed in the "dog-days," which drained her physically. It was with great joy that Elizabeth became untangled from the girls seminary to flee to the comforts of her sweet home. In one diary entry from this time we read: "August 22—Came home. Oh, so very happy! Dear, good home!"

A new chapter in Elizabeth's life became reality soon after. She began writing in her diary about a Mr. P who was soon to be her husband.

On April 16, 1845, Elizabeth Payson married Reverend George L. Prentiss, then the pastor of a church in New Bedford, Massachusetts. If ever there was a true calling on a life, then the life of a pastor's wife was with certainty a true calling for the newly married Elizabeth. She embraced life as a pastor's wife with a passionate devotion, as she ministered to the congregation with her great warm heart, ready sympathies, and her love for little children. Her kindness drew each one into her arms. Had she never given the world a line on the printed page, suffice it to say that she would have gone down in local church history as a genuine treasure and blessing to the congregation of her husband's church.

As the years passed by Elizabeth grew in confidence in her own talents and she became a leader in church enterprises. Her Bible readings before large female audiences won praise from those best qualified to be judges of such exercises. One eminent clergyman said it best: "I was impressed with her ability to combine rarest beauty and highest spirituality of thought with the uttermost simplicity of language and the plainest illustrations. Her conversation was like the mystic ladder which was set up on the earth, and the top of it reached to Heaven."

Life had been idyllic in her early home in New Bedford, tending to the congregation at the Mercer Street Presbyterian Church and enjoying the role of being the pastor's wife. She truly loved the household of faith and all the people in her husband's parish, and she also exuded tender sympathy for the irreligious. These qualities served her well in both marriage and ministry.

In 1846, her first child, Una, was born. Two years later, Edward came into the nursery, bringing much delight to the domestic scene. But in late 1851, the dark cloud of death swept fast upon the household, as first little Eddy, age three, and then baby Elizabeth, just 1 month old, left this world for heaven. Of baby Elizabeth she says, "I had her in my arms only twice. Once, the day before she died and once while she was dying. I never saw her little feet." A scrap of paper was found among her manuscripts entitled:

My Nursery, 1852

I thought that prattling boys and girls
  Would fill this empty room;
That my rich heart would gather flower
  From childhood's opening bloom.
One child and two green graves are mine,
  This is God's gift to me;
A bleeding, fainting, broken heart—
  This is my gift to Thee.

In 1853 she wrote *Little Susy's Six Birthdays*, reading each chapter as she went on to her husband, brother, and daughter. She had published nothing in the thirteen years prior to this time, although she was comforted by writing in journals. Sorrow had deepened the channels of thought; study, shrewd observation of the wider world to which she had been transferred, and association with scholars had filled the sluice-ways; love and loving made her life round and rich.

In 1854, *The Flower of the Family* was published. It had a cordial welcome in America, and was issued in France as *La Fleur de Famille,* and in Germany as *Die Perle der Famile.*

From this time on her pen was seldom idle and the prosperity of her books grew, but she confessed to a friend: "I long to have it do good. I never sat down to write without first praying that I might not be suffered to write anything that would do harm, and that, on the contrary, I might be taught to say what would do good. And it has been a great comfort to me that every word of praise I ever have received from others concerning it has been—'It will do good.' This I have had from so many sources that, amid much trial and sickness ever since its publication, I have had rays of sunshine creeping in, now and then, to cheer and sustain me."

Among Elizabeth's trials were the long illness of her baby—her fourth child, the deaths of valued friends, and—harder to bear than her own intense physical sufferings—growing solicitude on account of her husband's failing health.

Elizabeth wrote her most prominent work, *Stepping Heavenward,* in 1869. "Every word of that book was a prayer, and seemed to come of itself," she said. No doubt, it still is to hundreds of thousands of Christian women. The story of Katy's loves and mistakes, her aspirations and her despairs, her frolics and her bereavements of her steady progress in the way, the brightening and widening horizon, was read with tears and laughter. Sobbed thanksgivings for strength received by weary hearts through the practical spirituality of its teachings. (*Heroes of the Faith,* p. 207)

In 1858, Dr. Prentiss was compelled by declining health to resign the charge of his church, and he decided to take his whole family to Switzerland. They remained abroad two years. *Life and Letters* is Mrs. Prentiss' lively and earnest description of these traveling experiences.

Dr. Prentiss' health improved. Upon their return, he became the head and heart of a new church enterprise having for its object the formation of an uptown parish under the style of "The Church of the Covenant."

In 1867 she reorganized her household in the new parsonage in Thirty-fifth Street, selected the sight of and planned the cottage home in Dorset, England, wrote *Little Lou's Sayings,* and began *Stepping Heavenward,* penning whole chapters of it with her motherless little nephew on her lap. Soon after the completion of this book, and the first summer passed in the beloved Dorset retreat, Elizabeth watched as her sister-in-law died. Mrs. Steams, or "Anna," had been tenfold dearer than the ties of blood and name to Elizabeth for thirty years. There is nothing in English literature more touching than the letter describing this death scene. She describes it with only a few masterful lines that make readers feel as if they had watched and marveled at the transfiguration that preceded the woman's passing away.

We are reminded in perusing this and many other transcripts of Elizabeth's daily living and thinking of how "He Himself took our infirmities, and bore our diseases." The earnestness with which she threw herself into the joys and griefs of those she loved was a terrible strain upon her.

Her biographer says of her relentless activity of hand, heart, and brain, "Incessant work seemed to be in her case a sort of substitute for natural rest, and a solace for the want of it."

"I believe," she wrote a friend, "that God arranges our various burdens and fits them to our backs, and that He sets off a loss against a gain. I have to make it my steady object throughout each day so to spend time and strength as to obtain sleep enough to carry me through the next."

Yet the very same friend said of Mrs. Prentiss that she "seemed to be always in a flood of joy." When mind and body were faint to exhaustion, the unconquerable spirit made sport of her own evil plight.

In the *Life and Letters of Elizabeth Prentiss,* her husband George summarized the effect of her books: "Thus eminently fitted for her office of consoler, she exercised it, not only through her books, but also through her personal ministries in those large and widening circles which centered in her literary and pastoral life. Those who were favored with her friendship in times of sorrow found her a comforter indeed. Her letters, of which she was prodigal, were to many sore hearts as leaves from the tree of life. She did not expect too much from a sufferer. She recognized human weakness as well as Divine strength. But in all her attempts at consolation, side by side with her deep and true sympathy went the lesson of the harvest of sorrow."

In the last year of her life, Elizabeth was well aware that she was soon to be taken from this world, but "her magnetic influence held all hearts in breathless attention." At the close of her days she alluded to the trials of life and the shortness of them in light of eternity. "We are all passing away, one after another. And we should not allow ourselves to be troubled, lest when our time comes we may be afraid to die. Dying grace is not usually given until it is needed. Death to the disciple of Jesus is only stepping from one room to another and a far better room in our Father's house. And how little all the sorrows of the way will seem to us when we get to our home above!"

"As the end drew near," recalls her husband, "we all knelt together, and my old friend Dr. Poor commended the departing spirit to God, and invoked for us, who were about to be so heavily bereaved, the solace and support of the Blessed Comforter. The breathing at length became gentle, almost like that of one asleep, and her distressed look changed into a look of sweet repose."

At her graveside, her own sweet hymn, written from a bereaved heart, "More love, O Christ, to Thee," was sung to the glory of Christ, with whom she now enjoys eternal fellowship.

Scripture Application

HE WHO DWELLS IN THE SHELTER
OF THE MOST HIGH WILL REST
IN THE SHADOW OF THE ALMIGHTY.
I WILL SAY OF THE LORD,
"HE IS MY REFUGE AND MY FORTRESS,
MY GOD, IN WHOM I TRUST."
SURELY HE WILL SAVE YOU
FROM THE FOWLER'S SNARE
AND FROM THE DEADLY PESTILENCE.
HE WILL COVER YOU WITH HIS
FEATHERS, AND UNDER HIS WINGS
YOU WILL FIND REFUGE;
HIS FAITHFULNESS WILL BE
YOUR SHIELD AND RAMPART.
YOU WILL NOT FEAR THE TERROR OF
NIGHT, NOR THE ARROW THAT
FLIES BY DAY, NOR THE PESTILENCE
THAT STALKS IN THE DARKNESS, NOR
THE PLAGUE THAT
DESTROYS AT MIDDAY.

PSALM 91:1-6

PINK DIAMOND
I APPEAR TO BE A DIAMOND IN THE FIELDS OF THE LORD,
AND IT IS NOT BY ACCIDENT. I AM FEARFULLY AND WONDERFULLY MADE,
DESIGNED TO GIVE HIM ALL THE GLORY FOREVER AND EVER!
ANN MARIE REEVES' COMPASSION WAS LIKE THIS RADIANT FLOWER,
REFLECTING THE LOVE OF ALMIGHTY GOD.

Ann Maria Reeves Jarvis

1832–1905

Inspiration for Mother's Day

Ann Maria Reeves was born to the Reverend Josiah W. and Nancy Kemper Reeves on September 30, 1832 in Culpepper, Virginia. When she was still a child her father moved his family to Barbour County, in present day West Virginia, where he took up the pastorate of a Methodist Church in Philippi. Not much is known about the early years in Ann Maria's life, except that she had an extraordinary faith and a deep-rooted desire for community service.

In 1850 Ann married Granville E. Jarvis, son of the Philippi Baptist minister. Two years later, Granville and Ann moved to nearby Webster in Taylor County. Ann's heart was committed in service to her church and to those in need. She organized a series of what she called Mother's Day work Clubs in Webster and in other towns nearby to help improve health and sanitary conditions by inspecting bottled milk and food. The clubs also raised money to buy medicine for the poor and to hire women to care for mothers suffering from tuberculosis. By 1860 local physicians wholeheartedly supported the formation of clubs in many other towns.

Ann Maria's heart for the downtrodden and helpless would lead her to be right in the heart of the Civil War that literally raged around her. With the Baltimore and Ohio railroads nearby, it was only natural that Taylor County was deemed a strategic site for both the Union and Confederate Armies. Ann urged the Mother's Day Clubs to declare neutrality in order that they might aid both sides without being in harms way. Ann's actions enabled the clubs to treat the wounded and regularly feed and clothe the war weary soldiers who were stationed in the area. It was her faith that led her to bring a sense of calm and peace in a community being ripped asunder by political differences.

Ann's heart seemed big enough to love not only her large and growing family, but anyone who might be in need or suffering. Ann Marie worked tirelessly during the war despite dealing with the horrific tragedy of losing four of her darling children to disease. In fact Ann was to face death over and over again, as she lost eight of her twelve children before they could reach adulthood. Her love of her Lord Jesus Christ lifted her up and above the pain through her selfless act of service to others.

Toward the end of the war, the Jarvis family moved to the larger town of Grafton where Ann became involved in a peace-keeping measure between the returning soldiers from both the Confederate and Union Armies. Ann's heart was one of a mother, only wanting the young men to heal their inner wounds from battling with their brothers, which is what literally happened during the Civil War. In nearby Pruneytown, she organized a Mother's Friendship Day at the Courthouse bringing together the soldiers and numerous people from the area in an effort to mend political differences. Though many were fearful of the event erupting in violence, the Mothers' Friendship Day was a rousing success and became an annual event for several years thereafter.

Ann's husband Granville worked tirelessly to lead parishioners to build the Andrews Methodist Church in Grafton, and it was dedicated in 1873. Ann Maria's life still revolved around the church where she faithfully taught Sunday school for twenty-five years. When her husband died in 1902, Ann moved to Philadelphia to live with her son Claude and daughters Anna and Lillian. Three years later on May 9, 1905, she died at Bala-Cynwyd, just west of Philadelphia.

Ann Maria Reeves Jarvis lived a life of true service to others through her faith in Jesus Christ inspiring her daughter Anna to found Mother's Day in her honor.

Scripture Application

> HER CHILDREN ARISE AND CALL HER BLESSED;
> HER HUSBAND ALSO, AND HE PRAISES HER:
> "MANY WOMEN DO NOBLE THINGS,
> BUT YOU SURPASS THEM ALL."
>
> PROVERBS 31:28-29

BLUE PATCH

A COMPLEMENT TO THE MORE SPECTACULAR BLOOMS IN THE GARDEN,
I SURROUND THE OTHERS IN SUPPORT AND LIFT THEM UP IN THEIR
SPLENDOR. IT WAS IN THIS SPIRIT THAT ANN JARVIS LIVED HER LIFE,
GIVING OF SELF FOR A HIGHER PURPOSE, RELYING ONLY ON
THE GRACE OF GOD.

Anna Jarvis

1864–1948

Founder of Mother's Day

Anna Jarvis was born in Webster, Taylor County, West Virginia the ninth of eleven children born to Ann Maria and Granville Jarvis. When Anna was a year and a half old Anna's father moved the family to Grafton, four miles south of Webster where Anna spent her childhood and received her early education in public schools.

Anna's mother was a woman of great faith and character and left an indelible impression on her young daughter at an early age. During a class that her mother was teaching on "Mothers of the Bible," Anna, who at the time was twelve, listened intently to her mother's closing prayer at the conclusion of the class: "I hope that someone some time will found a memorial mothers day commemorating her for the matchless service she renders to humanity in every field of life. She is entitled to it." Anna recalled that prayer, even mentioning it at her mother's graveside service. Claude, Anna's brother exclaimed passionately, "By the grace of God, you shall have that Mother's Day."

Anna had tucked all of her mother's teachings, faith and love for her family in her heart as she grew into a thoughtful young woman. A bright pupil, Anna went on to further her education in what was then the Augusta Female Academy (now known as Mary Baldwin College). Upon completing her education at the Academy Mary returned to Grafton where she taught school for seven years.

Upon her father's passing in 1902, Anna, along with her sister Lillie and her mother, moved to Philadelphia to reside with her brother Claude. Sadly, within three years her beloved mother died leaving a deep void in her children's lives. Soon after her mother's death on May 9, 1905, Anna began an intense campaign to honor her mother's wish for a memorial day for all mothers.

The very next year on the anniversary of her mother's death, Anna and some friends reviewed the many accomplishments her mother had brought about through her Mother's Day Work Clubs that were established prior to the Civil War. Not long after this simple remembrance ceremony for her mother, Anna wrote to Mr. Norman F. Kendall of Grafton, petitioning him to organize a Mother's Day Memorial Committee by gleaning help from her mother's former co-workers at the Andrews Church. Mr. Kendall was more than happy to comply, and on May 12, 1907 a memorial service was held for Anna's mother Ann at the Andrew's Church. It was the second anniversary of her mother's death.

With great encouragement from her successful endeavor with the Andrews Church, Anna stepped out in enthusiasm as she set forth to engage legislators, executives and businessmen on both the local and national levels in establishing Mother's Day. Through hundreds of letters she sought to promote her program any way that she could think of, speaking anywhere that would allow, using her gift as a fluent speaker to try and influence her audiences. Most of her appeals fell on deaf ears, but Anna was not one to give up easily. The first real break that she rejoiced about came from her appeal to John Wanamaker, a great merchant and philanthropist in Philadelphia. It was his connections and clout that opened doors and made it possible for Anna's movement to gain momentum. On May 10, 1908, a fully-prepared program was held at the Andrews Methodist Episcopal Church in Grafton. A similar program was held later on in Philadelphia. The program marked the third anniversary of Ann Marie's death and her prayer of long ago now became reality with the observance of a general memorial for all mothers.

Anna had planned and prepared all of the details for the memorial service in Grafton, and Mr. L. Loar read a telegram that she had sent that defined the intent and purpose of the memorial:

"...To revive the dormant filial love and gratitude we owe to those who gave us birth. To be a home tie for the absent. To obliterate family estrangement. To create a bond of brotherhood through the wearing of a floral badge. To make us better children by getting us closer to the heart of our good mothers. To brighten the lives of good mothers. To have them know we appreciate them, though we do not show it as often as we ought...Mother's Day is to remind us of our duty before it is too late. This day is intended that we may make new resolutions for a more active thought to our dear mothers. By words, gifts, acts of affection, and in every way possible, give her pleasure, and make her heart glad every day, and constantly keep in memory Mother's Day; when you made this resolution, lest you forget and neglect your

dear mother, if absent from home write her often, tell her of a few of her noble good qualities and how you love her. A mother's love is new every day. God bless our mothers."

That day was just the beginning for Anna's dream of an official Mother's Day celebration. When the honorable Ira E. Robinson, a member of the congregation offered a resolution asking that Andrews Church adopt the memorial as a regular event, it was immediately approved. From that moment forward Mother's Day was celebrated each year at the Andrews Episcopal Church, which became known forevermore as the Mother Church of Mother's Day.

When Mr. Wanamaker opened his store auditorium in Philadelphia on the afternoon of May 10, 1908, an astounding 15,000 people lined up hoping to take part in the remembrance ceremony, when only 5,000 seats were available. Anna spoke eloquently to the crowd for an hour and ten minutes, truly reveling in the movement's success. There was much celebration for Anna and her friends that had been with her every step of the way as she sought recognition for all mothers.

Mother's Day quickly spread throughout the United States and even caught fire in Puerto Rico, Hawaii, Canada and Mexico. The observance was marked by the wearing of white and red carnations, which was deemed very appropriate by Miss Jarvis, who commented on the day by exclaiming "where it will end must be left for the future to tell. That it will girdle the globe seems now certain."

Governor William E. Glasscock of West Virginia issued a proclamation for the observance of Mother's Day on April 26, 1910. Then in May of 1914 Representative Heflin of Alabama and Senator Sheppard of Texas introduced a joint resolution, at the request of Anna Jarvis, naming the second Sunday in May as Mother's Day. This resolution was passed in both the House and Senate, and with President Woodrow Wilson's approval a proclamation was given by Secretary of State William Jennings Bryan. In the President's proclamation the flag was ordered to be displayed on Mother's Day on all government buildings in the U.S. and foreign possessions. Representative Heflin, co-author of the resolution, commented this way, "The flag was never used in a more beautiful and sacred cause than when flying above that tender, gentle army, the mothers of America."

Anna Jarvis enjoyed the beauty of Mother's Day, a tribute to her own blessed mother and to all mothers everywhere. However, when crass commercialism entered the picture, she was greatly distressed. She had used a vast amount of her own fortune to promote Mother's Day and now she was embroiled in the continued efforts of big business to exploit the day that she viewed as sacred. Though Anna tried to thwart these prolific money makers, it really was to no avail, and as much as she tried, she could not prevent the inevitable outcome. The commercialism of Mother's Day was here to stay.

In her later years Anna turned her attention to caring for her sister Lillie, who was now an invalid, and tending to her dear mother's grave. When her sister died in 1944 she was without family and in ill health, so her many friends placed her in the Marshall Square Sanitarium in West Chester, Pennsylvania. There Anna lived out the rest of her life. On November 24, 1948, she passed away at the age of 84 and was buried next to her beloved mother in West Laurel Hill Cemetery in Philadelphia. The Andrews Church rang their bell eighty-four times in remembrance of Anna, marking the years of her life spent in service to all mothers everywhere. And although Anna was never a mother, she is now lovingly known as the Mother of Mother's Day.

Scripture Application

"HONOR YOUR FATHER AND
MOTHER"—WHICH IS THE
FIRST COMMANDMENT
WITH A PROMISE—
"THAT IT MAY GO WELL
WITH YOU AND THAT
YOU MAY ENJOY LONG LIFE
ON THE EARTH."

EPHESIANS 6:2-3

FOURTH OF JULY FLOWER

THIS FLOWER SEEMS TO EXCLAIM TO THE WORLD, "I AM FULL OF LIFE!"
IT LOVES THE SUNSHINE BUT SUBMITS TO THE FATHER,
ACCEPTING THAT STORM CLOUDS AND RAIN MUST COME AS WELL.
THROUGH THE PROVISION OF GRACE, BETSY ROSS OVERCAME
THE STORM CLOUDS IN HER LIFE AS WELL.

Betsy Ross

1752–1836

Commissioned to Create a Flag

Elizabeth Griscom, also called Betsy, was born the eighth child into a large family of 17 children. Betsy was born into a fourth-generation Quaker family in Philadelphia, Pennsylvania, into the very heart of a country struggling to find its way, its destiny.

Betsy's parents, Rebecca James Griscom and Samuel, sent their bright, cheerful daughter to a Friend's (Quaker) public school where she spent eight hours a day dutifully learning reading, writing and the much needed instruction of a trade, most likely sewing. It was much to her father Samuel's credit that he thoughtfully apprenticed his daughter to a local upholsterer. In those times upholsterers did all manner of sewing, including flag making.

Betsy's faith was very important to her young life, which revolved around work and the prayer meetings held at the Quaker meeting house. The Quakers were very strict about not having anything to do with "other" denominations, so when Betsy fell in love with Episcopalian John Ross, she knew trouble would follow.

It was at her job that Betsy met and fell in love with fellow apprentice John, the son of an Episcopal Rector at Christ Church. Both John and Betsy knew what their love for each other would mean. Betsy would be "read out" in the Quaker meeting house in front of the whole congregation, meaning that she would be cut off financially and emotionally from both family and meeting house. So on a cold November night in 1773, 21-year-old Betsy eloped with her love, John Ross, taking a ferry across the Delaware River to Huggs Tavern, where they were married. Their marriage caused an irrevocable split from her family and just three years later John was disowned by his father, who was a loyalist (John was a staunch supporter of the Revolution). On an interesting note, because they married in New Jersey, their marriage license bore the name of then Governor William Franklin, son of Benjamin Franklin.

The thrifty couple began their own upholstery shop within the first two years of their marriage, and it was looked upon as a very bold decision indeed. Competition was tough because they could not count on Betsy's circle of friends. When she was "read out" of the Quaker community, Betsy became faithful to attend Christ Church along with her new husband John. It was there that the young couple could be found each week, sitting in pew 12, Betsy's heart intent on the encouragement she heard from the pulpit. Some Sundays, she might glimpse the tall, formidable figure of George Washington, America's new Commander in Chief, sitting in an adjacent pew.

It was in January of 1776 that Betsy and John truly felt the impact of what their fair city was going through. Philadelphia was torn apart by its citizens' split loyalties. Many showed their allegiance with Britain, protesting the mounting sentiment to the call to arms. Devout Patriots heeded the call, and John Ross was among them, joining the Pennsylvania Militia. It was while guarding an ammunition cache in mid-January 1776, Betsy's beloved husband was critically wounded in an explosion. In spite of her love and tender nursing, John died on the 21st and was buried in the cemetery at Christ Church.

Betsy relied heavily on her faith during this sad time in her life, and because she was now a widow she rejoined her Quaker meeting house for the support they now offered. But everything was not the same in the normally pacifist Quaker realm, even though the tenants of their faith forbid them to bear arms, many became "fighting Quakers" who supported the war effort. Betsy would often join them as they banded together to meet for encouragement and to rally other "Peaceful Quakers" to join their ranks.

After her dear husband's demise, Betsy continued her trade, sewing for the community of Philadelphia. In late May or early June of 1776, according to Betsy's account, she met with a committee of three that made the decision that led to the sewing of the nation's first flag. George Washington, George Ross and Robert Morris, met with the dedicated seamstress and appointed her to the task of making the design of the stars and stripes a reality.

In the summer of 1777 Betsy married sea captain Joseph Ashburn, and their wedding took place in Old Swedes Church in Philadelphia. The home of Joseph and Betsy was forcibly taken by the British army during that same year's infamous, bitter winter that besieged the ragged troops of the Continental Army at Valley Forge.

Betsy and Joseph were parents of two daughters, Zillah, who died in her youth, and Elizabeth. Betsy was soon to know more heartache when she learned from her old friend John Claypoole that her husband had died as a result of being imprisoned in the Old Mill Prison in England. John's firsthand account, for he had been a prisoner as well, was especially difficult for Betsy. Joseph's needless death occurred several months after the surrender of Cornwallis at Yorktown, Virginia, the last major battle of the Revolutionary War.

John Claypoole had been a devoted friend to Betsy, and in May of 1783 they wed. This, her third marriage, took place in none other than Christ Church. Betsy was very insistent that her new husband relinquish the call of the sea and take to employment that would be more fitting to a husband and father. John dutifully acknowledged her request and began his new work alongside Betsy in the upholstery trade. But soon after he took a job in the U.S. Customs House in Philadelphia were he worked to support their ever-expanding family of five little girls, Clarissa, Sidney, Susannah, Rachel, Jane and Harriet—who died at nine months of age. Because of their growing family, John sought out larger quarters for his brood and found a delightful home on Second Street in Philadelphia's mercantile district. But then, in 1817, John Claypoole passed away due to years of failing health.

If ever there was a time in Betsy's life to cling to her faith, it was now. It was her love for God that sustained her. She decided that at this point in her life she would never marry again. Instead Betsy turned her energy to her work, and after many years she brought members of her immediate family into the business alongside her. In 1827 she decided to retire and move into her daughter Susanna Satterthwaite's home in the remote suburb of Abington, Pennsylvania, just to the north of Philadelphia.

Betsy had seen many events in her lifetime, had known the love of three husbands, and had lost all three to death. Then there had been the challenges of being an outcast from her beloved faith, the peaceful Quakers, and the loss early in life of the support of her parents. The spirit of 1776 lifted her heart, and as a patriot, she heeded the call to use her gift and talents as a seamstress to create a symbol of a nation that yearned to be free. In 1834 Betsy watched as her beloved Free Quaker meeting house closed for good, understanding that the usefulness of the building was now all but gone forever.

Betsy's faith had sustained her lo, these many years, and after celebrating her 84th birthday on January 1, she breathed her last on January 30, 1836. Betsy Ross had lived the full life of daughter, wife, mother, business owner, patriot, and a believer in the Lord Jesus Christ. Betsy Ross takes a place in America's history as a great woman of courage and faith.

Scripture Application

> SURELY GOD IS MY HELP; THE LORD
> IS THE ONE WHO SUSTAINS ME.
>
> PSALM 54:4

FIRECRACKER MIX
ALIVE, BURSTING WITH ENERGY AND DETERMINATION,
NOTHING WILL STAND IN MY WAY OF ACCOMPLISHING WHAT I WAS
MEANT TO DO IN THE GARDEN. I THRIVE IN ADVERSITY AND
WHEN THE STORM CLOUDS GATHER, I STAND FIRM IN THE SHELTERING
ARMS OF THE CREATOR. MARY JANE PICKERSGILL TOOK UP HER CROSS
AND NEVER LOOKED BACK.

Mary Young Pickersgill

1776–1857

Designer of the Flag that Inspired "The Star-Spangled Banner"

Mary Young Pickersgill was born in Philadelphia, Pennsylvania, the youngest child in her family, in the midst of the turmoil of the Revolutionary War. Mary's mother, Rebecca Young was a flag maker and had made the Grand Unity flag that flew over General George Washington's headquarters on January 1, 1776.

When Mary turned 19 years of age, she married John Pickersgill at Old St. Paul's Church in Baltimore on October 2, 1795. Mary and John decided to move to Philadelphia where he accepted a position in England as a claims agent. Sadly, John died in London on June 14, 1805, and the young widow was left alone with her little daughter Caroline to support. (Mary and

John had three other children that did not survive their early life in childhood.) Faced with the daunting task of becoming both mother and father to little Caroline, she made the decision to move back to Baltimore to follow her mother's profession of flag making and the making of a ship's colors.

Mary did well in taking up the trade of flag making. She became quite skillful as a flag maker and soon garnered notable recognition for her abilities. Because of her reputation as a master flag maker, she was selected by Major George Armistead to sew a flag that would display 15 stars and 15 stripes, the number of states at that time. This was a critical time in young America's history as the war of 1812 was underway, and there was much talk of an anticipated attack by the British Fleet on Fort McHenry. It was 1813, the fighting had intensified and Major Armistead wanted an extra large flag that would bolster the spirits of the Baltimoreans. Major Armistead also knew that this amazing flag would cheer the troops on as they witnessed the flag flying in defiance of the British Fleet as they approached the formidable walls of Fort McHenry.

Mary and her 13-year-old daughter Caroline took to the task of creating this flag, a flag that was meant to rally courage and fly in the face of the aggressors of freedom. Time was of the essence in the construction of this mighty flag, and Mary and Caroline prayed that they would complete the task on time. The entire flag was sewn by hand with flat felled seams and tight stitching, so tight that not even an Atlantic gale would take it apart. It required four hundred yards of wool material. The finished flag measured 30 by 42 feet, and it was so large that the entire flag had to be assembled in a nearby malt house because no other place was large enough to allow them to maneuver the final construction. An astounding six weeks after accepting the assignment, Mary and Caroline lifted grateful eyes heavenward upon completion of this God-given task.

The flag was hoisted at the garrison of Fort McHenry as the British Fleet bombarded the fortress, demanding its surrender. Though the British ships continued with their heavy barrage for twenty-five solid hours, they were discouraged when the flag was still there.

Francis Scott Key witnessed this ferocious bombardment from a ship eight miles down the Patapsco River, so on the night of September 14, 1814, Key was inspired to write "The Star-Spangled Banner" that became America's National Anthem.

Mary Young Pickersgill had remained stalwart in her call to the challenge, and because of her faith and resolve, the flag she had made was still there. This flag can still be seen where it resides in the Smithsonian Institution's National Museum of American History.

After the war ended, Mary was able to continue work and to purchase a house. In her later years, Mary became president of the Impartial Humane Society, an organization founded to help find employment for women and to aid widows and deserted wives. She is thought to be the very first woman of Baltimore to begin a charitable foundation. Mary Young Pickersgill died on October 4, 1857 in her home. Her obituary described her as a woman of patriotism and love of country. It was Mary's love of God that sparked her heart to be a truly amazing woman of courage and faith.

Scripture Application

"DO NOT BE AFRAID;
YOU WILL NOT SUFFER SHAME.
DO NOT FEAR DISGRACE;
YOU WILL NOT BE HUMILIATED.
YOU WILL FORGET THE
SHAME OF YOUR YOUTH
AND REMEMBER NO MORE
THE REPROACH OF YOUR
WIDOWHOOD. FOR YOUR
MAKER IS YOUR HUSBAND—
THE LORD ALMIGHTY IS HIS
NAME—THE HOLY ONE
OF ISRAEL IS YOUR REDEEMER;
HE IS CALLED THE GOD
OF ALL THE EARTH."

ISAIAH 54:4-5

Resources

Corrie Ten Boom

The Hiding Place by Corrie Ten Boom & John Scherrill (Bantam Books, 1971); *Tramp for The Lord*, by Corrie Ten Boom with Jamie Buckingham (Revell, 1974). Wikipedia, the free encyclopedia.
The Hiding Place movie, released by the Billy Graham Evangelistic Association in 1975. Corrie Ten Boom museum www.corrietenboom.com; Holocaust Rescuers Bibliography: www.hearthasreasons.com.

Mother Teresa

Thomson Gale free Resources—Women's History Biographies; www.motherteresa.org.

Rossa Parks

Rosa and Raymond Parks Institute for Self Development; The American Civil Rights Movement; The Autobiography of Rosa Parks (1990) Beliefnet.com.
Other noted books of interest: *Don't Ride the Bus on Monday* by Louise Meriwether (1973) and Jo Ann Robinson's *The Montgomery Bus Boycott and the Women Who Started It* (1987). *Detroit News* (August 29, 1997 and September 28, 1997);

Sojourner Truth

Sojourner Truth Institute: (www.sojournertruthinstitute.org);
Spartacus School (www.spartacusschool.c,uk/usastruthe.htm);
The Free Dictionary (www.thefreedictionary.com); Ohio
Women in History (www.womeninhistoryohio.com).

Julia Ward Howe

www.greatwomen.org; Women of the Hall, www.juliawardhowe.org

Amy Carmichael

Website of the Dohnavur Fellowship (http://www.
dohnavurfellowship.org).
Books on Amy Carmichael: *A Chance to Die; the Life and Legacy
of Amy Carmichael* by Elisabeth Elliot (Grand Rapids, MI:
Fleming H. Revell Company, 1987). *A Life Abandoned to God*
by Sam Wellman (Barbour Publishing, 1998).
Amy Carmichael: To Live Our Songs (http://www.
inversionfellowship.org/docs/amy-carmichael.pdf).

Marian Anderson

Liberty Foursquare Church (www.libertyfoursquarechurch); The
Marian Anderson Historical Society (www.mariananderson.
org); Penn Special Collection Marian Anderson: A Life In Song
(www.library.upeen.edu/edu/exhibitbm/andersom); Kennedy
Center (www.kennedy-center.org).

Pandita Rambai

Pandita Rambai, The Story of Her Life by Helen S. Dyer, 1911;
www.answers.com.

Mahalia Jackson

Women in History. Mahalia Jackson biography. Lakewood Public
Library; Mahalia Jackson—Famous Christians in History;
Mahalia Jackson—the World's Greatest Gospel Singer; Rock
and Roll Hall of Fame and Museum Inductee: Mahalia Jackson
Further reading: *Just Mahalia Baby* by Laurraine Goreau (Waco:
Word Books, 1975); *Got to Tell It Mahalia Jackson Queen of
Gospel* by Jules Schwerin, 1992 (sound recording Cleveland
Public Library). *Mahalia Jackson* by Charles Wolfe (New
York: Chelsea House, 1990).

Aimee Semple McPherson

Bibliography: *Aimee Semple McPherson: Everybody's Sister* by
Edith Waldvogel Blumhofer (Grand Rapids: W. B. Eerdmans
Publishing Company, 1993); *Sister Aimee: The Life of Aimee
Semple McPherson* by Daniel Mark Epstein (New York:
Harcourt Brace, 1993); *Aimee: Life Story of Aimee Semple
McPherson* by Aimee Semple McPherson (Los Angeles:
Foursquare Publications, 1979).

Henrietta Mears

What the Bible Is All About by Dr. Henrietta C. Mears with a
foreword by Billy Graham.
*Websites: www.SheLovesGod.com; www.InTouch.com; www.
HistoricalRenewal.org; www.History'sWomen.org.*

Gladys Aylward

History of Gospel Song and Hymn Writers by J. H. Hall, New
York: Fleming H. Revell Company, @ 1914, The New York
Times, *Heroes of the Faith*, Bridge Logos Publishing Company
Websites: www.nyise.org
www.chi.Gospelcom.net
www.chi.Gospelcom.net

www.intouch.org
www.believersweb.org
www.cyberhymnal.org

Eliza Shirley

The Salvation Army Website: www.usc.salvationarmy.org/
editorial/elizashirley.htm *Hallelujah Lass* by Wendy Lawton
(Moody Press, 2004).

Fanny Crosby

History of Gospel Song and Hymn Writers by J. H. Hall (New
York: Fleming H. Revell Company, 1914; *The New York
Times, Heroes of the Faith* by Gene Fedele (Orlando: Bridge-
Logos, 2003).
Websites: www.nyise.org; www.tlogical.net; www.chi.Gospelcom.
net; www.chi.Gospelcom.net; www.intouch.org; www.
believersweb.org; www.cyberhymnal.org.

Susannah Spurgeon

www.spurgeon.org, *Mrs. C.H.S. Spurgeon* by Charles Ray.

Anne Hutchinson

www.rootsweb.com, www.greatwomen.org
www.annehutchinson.com
www.spartacus.shoolnet.co.uk.

Martha Washington

White House History of First Ladies; *Prayer, Power & Petticoats*
by Sue E. Tennant (Orlando: Bridge-Logos, 2004); *Lady
Washington* by Dorothy Clarke Wilson (NY: Doubleday &
Company, 1984); Martha Washington picture—watercolor on

ivory, painted by James Peale in 1796; Mount Vernon Ladies
Association.

Dale Evan

Happy Trails (Dale Evan's autobiography); *Growing Up with Roy
& Dale* by Roy Rogers, Jr., with Karen Ann Wojahn (1986);
Angel Unaware.

Elizabeth Prentiss

Life and Letters of Elizabeth Prentiss by George L. Prentiss, A.D.F.
Randolph (New York: Springfield Republican). *Heroes of the
Faith* by Gene Fedele (Orlando: Bridge-Logos Publishing
Company, 2003).

Ann Maria Reeves Jarvis

www.answers.com; www.culture.org

Anna Jarvis

West Virginia Archives & History; www.rootsweb.com; www.
peopleoffaith.com.

Betsy Ross

www.ushistory.org; www.foundingfathersinfo.org

Mary Young Pickersgill

Maryland's Women's Hall of Fame.
Related topics: Battles: Battle of Baltimore; Documents;
The Star-Spangled Banner